Our Soldiers' Stories:
Kern County Goes to War—From the Beaches of Normandy to the Deserts of Iraq

Dr Craig W.H. Luther

(Foreword by Alex Athans)

ISBN Number: 978-1-7366114-7-0

Book layout and design: *Sara Olsher*

All proceeds from sales of this book will go to the following three organizations:

a. The Charles B. Burdick Military History Project (San Jose State University)
b. The Major Jason E. George VFW Post 12114 (Tehachapi, CA)
c. The Portrait of a Warrior Galley (Bakersfield, CA)

This book is dedicated to all who serve, or have served, our country, but especially to those who paid for their service with their lives. May the stories in this modest little book help to forever sustain our memory of their sacrifice.

"If a man hasn't discovered something that he will die for, he isn't fit to live." **(Martin Luther King, Jr.)**

"We sleep peaceably in our beds at night only because rough men stand ready to do violence on our behalf." **(George Orwell)**

"Out of every one hundred men, ten shouldn't even be there, eighty are just targets, nine are the real fighters, and we are lucky to have them, for they make the battle. Ah, but the one, one is a warrior, and he will bring the others back." **(Heraclitus)**

"His name and fame are the birthright of every American citizen. In his youth and strength, his love and loyalty he gave—all that mortality can give. He needs no eulogy from me or from any other men. He has written his own history and written it in Red on his enemy's breast." **(General Douglas MacArthur on the American Soldier)**

Table of Contents

FOREWORD

Between the covers of this book is a collection of 25 stories of the men and women who answered the call of duty for their country to help protect our precious freedoms and our way of life.

The idea of this book took hold when a local newspaper ("The Loop Newspaper") contacted author Dr. Craig Luther, who lives in the community, to write articles about local veterans for publication in the newspaper. The stories were well received by the citizens of Tehachapi and the surrounding communities. I have read all the stories and must compliment Dr. Luther on his achievement. Dr. Luther is an internationally recognized World War II historian who has written eight books about the war, among them several books addressing Adolf Hitler's attack on Russia in June 1941. As more than one book reviewer has pointed out, Dr. Luther's research for his books is second to none. He has been interviewed for programs on World War II on the History Channel, lectured at Marine Corps University and National Defense University, and is often a guest on the Terry Maxwell Show (KNZR 1560 AM).

The veterans' stories in this volume cover World War II, the Korean War, the Vietnam War, and the recent conflict in Iraq. The city of Tehachapi, surrounding communities, and Kern County as a whole should be very proud of its veterans. Kern County has been home to many veterans throughout the years. Within the pages of this book are the stories of our soldiers who fought in the Battle of the Bulge during World War II, the brutal battle at the Chosen Reservoir in Korea, the Tet offensive during the Vietnam War, and took part in combat against al Qaeda terrorists in Baghdad and Ramadi during the Iraq War. The stories also include accounts of two brave nurses who served in Vietnam at the height of the war there.

In Bakersfield, California, there is a Portrait of a Warrior Gallery, located in an inconspicuous building on Eye Street. Among the 27 portraits that hang on the gallery walls—all of Kern County soldiers killed in the war on terror since September 11, 2001—are those of Adam Zanutto, Alberto Garcia Jr., and Jason E. George, who gave all. Their stories are also in this book.

Ten years ago, a new Veterans of Foreign Wars (VFW) Post 12114 was created in Tehachapi, California, to honor Major Jason E. George, a local resident and a hero who lost his life in Iraq in 2009 and was the first veteran to be interred at the Bakersfield National Cemetery. His mother was elated that a VFW was named to honor her son. She stated that now her son's name will live on forever. On Memorial Day Weekend, 2021, she presented to VFW Post 12114 Jason's West Point ceremonial sword.

Dr. Luther has often stated that he feels truly honored to have written these stories and completed this book. It has given him the opportunity to meet and get to know many veterans and their families. This undertaking has been a most rewarding experience for him. Craig Luther, I thank you for your efforts and your expertise in writing these stories. They have given us insight into what our veterans have so selflessly accomplished for our country's freedom and liberty over three generations.

The widow of Major Brent Taylor recently stated, "When the American Soldier wakes up every morning and puts on the uniform, they are telling us that they are willing to die for you today."

God Bless the men and women who have served, as well as those who are currently serving in our military.

Alex Athans
"B" Battery, Ist Battalion, 83rd Artillery (Vietnam)
Tehachapi, California

September 22, 2021

Preface

I must begin with a confession. This book project did not begin with me; in other words, it does not belong to an original idea of mine. The original idea—to write and publish stories of local veterans—belongs to Claudia Needham-Baker, owner/publisher of Tehachapi's wonderful community newspaper, "The Loop Newspaper."

My wife, Therese, has worked at "The Loop Newspaper" for about two years now, and she and I have both contributed occasional pieces to the paper. Sometime, late last year, Claudia asked my wife to ask me a question: Would I be willing to research and write articles for the paper on local military veterans?

My initial response to Claudia's query was . . . hardly ennobling. I am an author of books on World War II and, in 2020, after much concerted effort, I had published two new books on my favorite topic (Adolf Hitler's invasion of Soviet Russia in June 1941). Hence, I was in no mood to begin another writing project. Simply put, I was tired. Yet how could I say "no" to our military veterans, for whom I have such admiration and respect? Of course, I could not say "no," so my first article in the paper—about U.S. Navy veteran Jed Hannan—appeared in the November 7-21, 2020 issue.

With the enthusiastic support of many patriots in Tehachapi and Kern County, I began to learn more about our local servicemen and women and their amazing stories that span more than three generations. Some were deceased, but their stories still very much alive. Others were thankful to know that neither they, nor their sacrifices to our country, had been forgotten, for a local military historian wanted to learn more about them—about why they served when so many did not, or would not; about their stories, which in many ways were strikingly similar, yet also utterly unique. (That may seem to pose a paradox of sorts, but after you read the articles, you will understand.)

Following my article about Jed Hannan, I continued to research, write, and publish an article on a local veteran in just about every edition of "The Loop Newspaper" (every two weeks). After finishing six or seven of the articles, I came to an epiphany of sorts. I began to realize what a unique experience it was to learn about these glorious men (and women, too), who had done so much for all of us but all too often had been forgotten and ignored, even shunned. And I must again confess—before I began these articles I had not the slightest idea just how many extraordinary stories of sacrifice, heroism, hope, fear, and death were hiding among us in plain sight.

So I continued to network, to meet new veterans, to write new stories. And in less than a year, I had completed the 25 stories that fill this little volume. The stories cover a lot of historical terrain—from the bloody sands of Omaha Beach in Normandy, France, to the arctic cold of the Chosin Reservoir in North Korea; from the jungles and rice paddies of Vietnam to the harsh climes of Iraq.

As a professional military historian, I have spent more than half a century researching and writing about war. As a youngster, I was captivated by our Civil War, and particularly seduced by the popular

Civil War histories of the late Bruce Catton. As I grew older, I developed an interest in German military operations in World War II, a subject that to this day has remained my primary field of interest. Over the decades, I have corresponded with, or personally interviewed, many dozens of German WWII veterans, among them men who had gone through combat in Normandy in 1944 and, more recently—by that I mean since about 2001—former German soldiers who had taken part in the titanic struggle between Hitler's Germany and Stalin's Russia.

I only bring all that up to make a point, and it is this: Never in my career as a military historian have I been more moved, more shaken, more "gobsmacked" (if I may employ a crass but quite appropriate idiom) than by the stories I've been told, and shared with "The Loop" readers, over the past year. And it is because these stories are so rich, so excruciatingly human, that I decided to assemble them into this book.

So, dear reader, let me petition you with this eager plea: Share these remarkable stories with others. Share them particularly with young people, too many of whom have been indoctrinated in our high schools and colleges to disparage the men and women who have so selflessly served our nation. Talk to others about our active duty military, about our veterans, and don't let anyone ever forget this unassailable truth:

"We sleep peaceably in our beds at night only because rough men stand ready to do violence on our behalf." **(George Orwell)**

Dr. Craig W.H. Luther

Tehachapi, California

September 15, 2021

PART ONE

World War II

CHAPTER 1

John Grenek: From Omaha Beach to the Rhine River

John Grenek, grew up in Minneapolis, Minnesota. In January 1940, having just finished high school, he enlisted in the Minnesota National Guard. In 1941, the National Guard was federalized, and his unit dispatched to Camp Claiborne, Louisiana. Following basic training, he was transferred to Fort Dix, New Jersey, from where he shipped out to England in January 1942. As part of the first contingent of American soldiers to arrive in the United Kingdom, Grenek was initially assigned to a British Army regiment.

After sustaining a broken ankle in a training exercise, he spent a few months recuperating at a hospital in Dublin, Ireland. Once healthy, he was assigned to the 29th Infantry Division (29 ID) and, on June 6, 1944—that iconic day more than 77 years ago still emblazoned in the hearts and minds of Americans as "D-Day"—he landed with the third or fourth wave on Omaha Beach. Yet D-Day was also "the Longest Day" for the G.I.s who struggled valiantly ashore at Omaha, greeted by sheets of fire from German machine gun nests, mortars, and heavy

American soldiers seek cover behind the sea wall on Omaha Beach on D-Day.

weapons concealed with Teutonic precision on the bluffs above the beach: By day's end, as many as 1500 American soldiers lay dead in the blood-soaked sand, or floating in the water among the Germans' diabolical beach obstacles.

In the weeks and months following that gruesome prelude to the liberation of western Europe from Nazi tyranny, Grenek and his fellow "29ers" took part in the push through France and into Germany, seeing almost continuous combat until V-E (Victory Europe) Day on May 8, 1945. The website of the 29th Division Association offers graphic insight into the brutal fighting experienced by the division:

"The 29th entered Germany on October 1, 1944. . . For more than a month, the division engaged in frustrating positional warfare as the weather deteriorated sharply and an ammunition shortage worsened to a critical level. Fully recovered from the debacle in Normandy, the Germans gave little ground and inflicted heavy casualties each time the 29ers launched an attack. On November 16, 1944, the 29th Division joined in one of the largest U.S. Army offensives of the war to date as a component of the Ninth Army. The goal was to smash through the German lines in the Rhineland, cross the Roer River and drive on to the Rhine by Christmas 1944. In three weeks of brutal combat, however, [29 ID] only managed to advance nine miles. The minuscule German towns through which the 29th fought would be remembered by the 29ers as some of the most brutal fighting they experienced in World War II. Further, as cold and wet weather set in, the 29th Division lost hundreds of men due to exposure and trench foot." (https://29thdivisionassociation.com)

Eventually pushing its way deeper into Germany, the division crossed the Rhine River on March 31, 1945. For the next five weeks, it mopped up scattered pockets of enemy resistance and, on May 2nd, elements of the 29 ID encountered the Soviet 6th Guards Cavalry Division on the Elbe River. The Americans and Red Army men greeted one another enthusiastically, exchanging hats, weapons, and other items of military memorabilia. Six days later, the war was over.

All told, more than 20,000 men of the 29th Infantry Division fell in battle, with many tens of thousands more wounded. In fact, of the 60-plus U.S. Army divisions that took part in the European campaign, only one other division had more losses. For his sterling military service,

Advance Guard of 29th Infantry Division entering St. Lo. 1944.

Grenek was awarded five Bronze Stars (source: Aerotechnews, 3 Nov 2017, updated 22 Mar 2021). He was honorably discharged from the Army in April 1945.

Yet, just a month prior to his discharge, Grenek had gotten "hitched!" Here's the story, which, of course, was repeated many times over throughout the war in Europe: One day while in England, before deploying to France, at the American Red Cross in Birmingham, a fetching English girl named Jane caught his eye. Grenek married her on March 6, 1945, and brought her back to the States.

After the war, and before moving to Tehachapi, Grenek was a real estate broker in Orange County. On June 6, 1994, the 50th anniversary of the D-Day invasion, he and Jane toured the former battlefields of Normandy, where the French government awarded him the 50th Anniversary "Legion of Honor" Medal. (Note: This author was also in Normandy on June 6, 1994, as a tour guide for veterans of the 5th Infantry Division, which had landed in France in early July 1944. He will never forget sitting in the bleachers erected on Omaha Beach across from President Bill Clinton, the Queen of England, and most of the leaders of the Free World—50 years from that very day when the fate of Hitler's "1000-year Reich" had been forever sealed.)

In addition to visiting Normandy, Grenek had the privilege, as a World War II veteran, of being on the first Honor Flight conducted by Honor Flight Kern County, "a nonprofit organization that flies hundreds of aging vets to Washington, D.C—all expenses paid—where they participate in a whirlwind tour of the great war memorials in our nation's capital." (Bakersfield Californian, June 6, 2016, updated September 13, 2016)

Grenek never forgot the brave young men who served at his side during the struggle for freedom against Hitler's Germany, but who never made it home. In an interview with a local television reporter on Memorial Day, 2016, he said: "I had so many of my friends and buddies who fell along side me. And I'm here to honor them."

John G. Grenek passed away peacefully on November 26, 2019, at his home in Tehachapi. He was 98 years old.

With his wife of more than 70 years and son, John Grenek, Jr., at his side, he was laid to eternal rest with Honors at the Bakersfield National Cemetery.

John Grenek late in his life. Photo provided.

CHAPTER 2

Emery Hubbard: Anti-Tank Trooper (Battle of the Bulge)

Emery Hubbard was inducted into the military on December 9, 1943. After basic training, he was assigned as a cannoneer to an anti-tank (AT) company in the 75th Infantry Division at Camp Breckinridge, Kentucky. His division shipped out from the New York Port of Embarkation in mid-November 1944, reaching England eight days later. Following additional training, the division landed in France on December 13, 1944.

Three days later (December 16th), Adolf Hitler launched a powerful, surprise offensive through the snow-covered, densely forested Ardennes region between Belgium and Luxembourg in a final, desperate bid to turn the tide against his British and American adversaries. To help stem the German advance, Hubbard's 75th Infantry Division was rushed to the front and engaged in tenacious defensive combat.

On the cold Christmas night of December 25, 1944, 20-year-old

Private First Class Hubbard was on sentry duty, when German forces advanced toward his company, positioning a machine gun (MG) in a nearby house. Hubbard, who had acquired a Thompson submachine gun from a motorcycle messenger, volunteered along with five other men to mount an assault on the German MG post. The assault failed, and four of the men were killed. Undaunted, Hubbard and the other survivor (a sergeant) returned with an anti-tank gun and knocked out the German machine-gun nest.

Following the Allied victory in the Battle of the Bulge, the 75 ID was soon battling its way into Germany. In mid-April 1945, with the war approaching its end, the division was pulled out of the line for rest and rehabilitation. It was then assigned security and military government duties in Westphalia, a region in northwestern Germany.

Hubbard, who returned to the United States as a master sergeant, was discharged from the military in March 1946. His impressive collection of combat medals included the Bronze Star, Combat Infantry Badge,

Column of 289th Infantry Regiment (75 ID) advancing during Battle of the Bulge.

Bronze Star Medal of WWII.

European Theater of Operations (ETO) Medal with three battle stars, and the German Occupational Medal.

In subsequent years he completed his education, graduating from both Bakersfield College and Brigham Young University. He also attended the National University of Mexico and became fluent in Spanish. He eventually went to work for the Ken County Sheriff's Department as a deputy sheriff and sergeant. He spent the last 20 years of his professional life working for the Welfare Department as an investigator.

On March 24, 1967, Hubbard had married his second wife, Alice—a marriage that brought forth two children (both Emery and Alice also had a child with their first spouses). As Alice recalled, her husband rarely talked about his war experiences; however, "he always told a couple of stories," she said: "On one occasion, Emery was in a foxhole, he and the others were under artillery fire. A couple of soldiers jumped in his foxhole because they felt safe with him. He was a trusted soldier and a very religious man. Another time, a superior officer, who was in a jeep, said he was driving out to the front to see where his men were. So Emery jumped in front of the jeep and said, 'No, no, Sir! You don't want to go out there!' But the officer said, 'Get out of my way, soldier, I'm going through!' Well, the officer didn't make it back. Those were the only two things he ever really talked about."

When her husband turned 60, Alice sent him on vacation to all the spots where he had served in Europe during the war. Later, they traveled together to Europe and visited the battlefields of the Battle of the Bulge. They also began to regularly attend the meetings of WWII veterans organizations, on occasion accompanied by Bill Jasper (see next story); as a result, Hubbard began to open up more about his wartime experiences. In May 2004, the couple visited the National World War II Memorial in Washington D.C. shortly after it had opened (the memorial is dedicated to the 16,000,000 who served in our armed forces during WWII and the 406,000 who perished protecting our freedoms).

Emery M. Hubbard passed away peacefully in Tehachapi on March 24, 2017—it was their wedding anniversary; they had been married for exactly 50 years.

When I asked Alice what she remembered most about her husband, she didn't hesitate: "Emery loved people. He was very gentle, quiet. He loved his children and grandchildren. And he loved the Boy Scouts of America. He was a scoutmaster for many years and made sure our two boys attended the scouting jamborees on the east coast. I might add that Emery was also quite adventuresome; for his 65th birthday he went sky diving!"

It should also be pointed out that, in his later years, he was active with the Tehachapi Senior Center and was dedicated to serving the Latter-Day Saints Church.

Emery: Thank you so much for your wonderful service to our country. You will be sorely missed. We need more men like you in our world.

Emery Hubbard's Grave Site. Photo Provided.

CHAPTER 3

Henry Martinez & Arthur Jasper: Sniper & Combat Engineer (Battle of the Bulge)

Barely 18 years old, Henry Martinez joined the U.S. Army in June 1944, just as the Anglo-American invasion of Normandy, France, was getting underway. Following just four weeks of basic training, he was on his way to Europe to join the 28th Infantry Division (110th Battalion, Company "B"). The division had departed the United States on October 8, 1943, and crossed the Atlantic, arriving in South Wales to begin training for the impending invasion of France. On July 22, 1944, seven weeks after the D-Day landings, the division arrived in Normandy. The men of the 28th Division fought their way through France and, on August 28th, entered Paris and were given the honor of marching down the Champs-Elysées the next day to celebrate the liberation of Paris.

While it is unclear when Henry arrived in France, he may very well have been with the division when it marched into Paris. Eventually, his 28th Division made it to the Ardennes forest, which ran through Belgium and Luxembourg. Although this densely forested region

German tank destroyed during the fighting in the Bulge.

was close to the German frontier, it was considered largely safe from attack and thus used as a rest area for American troops and as a place to "break in" green troops.

That all changed, however, on December 16, 1944, when Adolf Hitler launched a desperate last ditch effort to push through to the Allied port of Antwerp, split the British and American forces, and force the Western Allies to settle for a negotiated peace with Nazi Germany. The entire divisional front of Henry's 28th Division was struck by a powerful German tank army. Fighting back doggedly against superior enemy forces, and throwing all available personnel into the fray, the 28th succeeded in disrupting the enemy's timetable before pulling back on December 22nd to refurbish its badly mauled formations.

During the Battle of the Bulge, Henry distinguished himself by making solo trips at night behind German lines to gather vital intelligence, while also engaging in combat as a sniper and .50 caliber machine-gun operator. The winter of 1944/45 in northern Europe was quite harsh. Henry and his fellow soldiers hunkered down in foxholes they had carved out of the ice, tossing in leaves to gain a small measure of protection from the arctic cold. On one of Henry's forays behind enemy lines, he suddenly found himself face to face with a German soldier; however, instead of making use of their weapons, both men reasoned that, in this case, discretion was the better part of valor! They simply went their separate ways without a shot being fired.

The Battle of the Bulge concluded in late January 1945, with the badly attrited German forces staggering back in defeat. By the end of the war in Europe, Henry, for his distinguished service in the European theater, had garnered the Bronze Star, Purple Heart and the French Croix de Guerre. Due to injuries sustained, he spent two months in a European hospital before being transported to Fort Lewis, Washington, to complete his recovery. All told, his 28th Division experienced 196 days of combat, sustaining nearly 17,000 battle casualties, including 2316 killed in action.

Although small in stature, Henry Martinez was a tenacious warrior who loved his country and his fellow soldiers dearly. A longtime resident of Tehachapi, he passed away on January 9, 2017 at the age of 91.

Arthur William ("Bill") Jasper enlisted in the U.S. Army in early 1943 at the age of 17. Like Henry Martinez, he was soon shipping out for the European theater of operations, where he would see combat with General George S. Patton's Third Army. Initially, Bill served in an infantry division, however, sometime before the Battle of the Bulge he volunteered for transfer to the Army Air Forces (AAF). Yet a short time after reporting to the AAF, the Germans launched their Ardennes offensive. The infantry company with which Bill had previously served was virtually wiped out by the overwhelming enemy assault. Needing replacements at the front lines, Bill was rapidly transferred out of the AAF and assigned to a unit of combat engineers.

U.S. Army combat engineers played an indispensable role in the Second World War. For example, they facilitated the movement of friendly forces by breaching enemy obstacles, eliminating enemy strongpoints, minesweeping, and building roads and bridges. They slowed the advance of enemy forces through such actions as laying mines, constructing fortifications for defending friendly forces, or blowing up bridges to impede enemy progress. Combat engineers were also trained to fight as infantrymen and often did so during crisis situations on the field of battle.

While it is unclear which combat engineering unit Bill was assigned to, his activities would have embraced at least some of those outlined above. During the Battle of the Bulge, Bill serendipitously survived an incident that could have easily led to his death: Due to the arctic cold, Bill and his fellow engineers sheltered three to a foxhole. Every so often, the men in the foxhole rotated. On one occasion, Bill rotated

Henry Martinez later in life. Photo provided.

out of the middleman position to being on the left. No sooner had he done this than the new man in the middle was shot dead by a German sniper—just another example of how survival in war often comes down to luck, physics, or God's unknowable plan.

Bill survived World War II and served in the Army reserves until 1965, retiring with the rank of major. In 1954, after completing his undergraduate studies, he earned a doctoral degree in agriculture from Cornell University, New York. Bill went on to become Director of Marketing for the American Farm Bureau Federation and President and General Manager of West Coast Egg Producers. Bill, in fact, was the one who coined a "spiffy" phrase anyone of us "old-timers" should readily recall: "the incredible, edible egg!" In 2004, he journeyed back to Belgium for the 60th Anniversary of the Battle of the Bulge. It was a moving experience for Bill, who was deeply touched by the young children who approached him and thanked him for what he had done to liberate their country from tyranny.

Bill was also one of just six veterans who founded the Major Jason E. George, VFW Post 12114, some 10 years ago. A longtime resident of Stallion Springs, Bill Jasper passed away on June 7, 2012. And

U.S. Combat engineers search for mines.

Tehachapi, and America, lost another irreplaceable hero.

Henry and Bill—Although you are no longer with us, you are not forgotten. And we will never forget the heroism with which you served our great country!

Arthur William ("Bill") Jasper. Photo provided.

CHAPTER 4

John Byron Pruden, Sr.: Navy Destroyer Fends off Kamikaze Attacks

John was born on January 28, 1917, in Globe (Gila County) Arizona to John and Willhelmina Farnham Pruden. He came of age during the hardships of the Great Depression, serving for a year with the Civilian Conservation Corps building fire roads in southern California (including in the San Gabriel Mountains).

He enlisted in the Navy in 1935. While no information was available about his early years in the Navy, during World War II, he first served aboard the USS Dewey (DD-349), a Farragut-class destroyer escort. On December 18, 1944, while supporting the invasion of the Philippines, the Dewey sustained heavy damage in a typhoon, an ordeal that ended with the battered vessel still afloat, but having lost all power, listing more than 75 degrees, and losing her number one stack (torn off and thrown against the boat deck!).

Although the USS Dewey was repaired and returned to service in early 1945, John (now a Lieutenant Junior Grade Assistant Gunnery Officer) was reassigned to the USS Hadley (DD-774), a new

The USS Hugh W. Hadley (DD-774). Photo provided.

Sumner-class destroyer boasting a number of improvements over the standard Fletcher-class destroyers, among them twin 5-inch/38 caliber gun mounts, dual rudders, additional anti-aircraft guns, and an advanced fire-control system (for more efficient gunnery operations).

In the spring of 1945, the Hadley was operating off the coast of Okinawa, supporting the invasion of this Japanese home island that had begun on April 1 and signified the largest amphibious assault by U.S. and Allied forces in the Pacific Theater during WWII. It was during this time that the Hadley, like so many other U.S. and Allied warships, came under attack from Japanese kamikaze aircraft, which conducted desperate suicide attacks on our naval vessels in the closing stages of the Pacific campaign (some 3800 kamikaze pilots would lose their lives, along with more than 7000 Allied naval personnel).

Which brings us to that tragic yet unforgettable day—May 11, 1945. Fighting alongside the USS Evans (Fletcher-class destroyer, DD-552), the Hadley made history on this day, shooting down 23 kamikazes in a 95-minute air/sea battle while enduring five hits from planes and bombs and suffering 151 casualties (including 30 killed in action). The 23 kamikazes shot down by the Hadley established a U.S. Navy record for a single engagement and earned the valiant ship the sobriquet "The Champion Kamikaze Killer."

For her unparalleled performance, the USS Hadley was awarded a Presidential Unit Citation, which describes the events of May 11 in graphic detail:

"CITATION: For extraordinary heroism and action as Fighter Direction Ship on Radar Picket Station Number 15 during an attack by approximately 100 enemy Japanese planes, forty miles northwest of the Okinawa Transport Area on 11 May 1945. Fighting valiantly against waves of hostile suicide and dive-bombing planes plunging toward her in all directions, the USS HUGH HADLEY sent up relentless barrages of anti-aircraft fire during one of the most furious air-sea battles of the war. Repeatedly finding her targets, she destroyed twenty planes, skillfully directed the Combat Air Patrol in shooting down at least 40 others and, by her vigilance and superb battle readiness avoided damage herself until subjected to a coordinated attack by ten Japanese planes. Assisting in the destruction of all ten of these, she was crashed by one bomb and three suicide planes with devastating effect. With all engineering spaces flooded and with a fire raging amidships, the gallant officers and men of the HUGH W. HADLEY fought desperately against insurmountable odds and, by their indomitable determination, fortitude and skill, brought the damage under control, enabling their ship to be towed to port and saved. Her brilliant performance in the action reflects the highest credit upon the HUGH W. HADLEY and the United States Naval Service."

In addition to the coveted Presidential Unit Citation, the Hadley's crew was awarded 121 Purple Hearts and 20 other individual medals. One of those medals was a Silver Star awarded to Lieutenant Pruden for his leadership and courage: He had led a fire-fighting party that subdued a fire resulting from the kamikaze attacks.

After the war, John elected to make a career in the Navy. In the late 1940s, he served aboard heavy cruisers at several stations on both the east and west coasts (much to the dismay, one might add, of his three young children, who found themselves constantly uprooted as they moved from place to place!) As his surviving son, John H. Pruden (also a proud Navy veteran) recalled: "My father was so proud to serve in the Navy, and he did whatever the Navy asked him to do. He had gone through the depression; you couldn't find a job in the 1930s. And the Navy helped him to complete his education and took care of

Japanese kamikaze pilot goes down with his plane.

and supported his family.

John served in the Korean War with the heavy cruiser USS Los Angeles. Later, the Navy sent him to college, and he graduated from the University of Washington. He also attended the War College and the Defense Language Institute at the Presidio of Monterey. After more than 22 years of distinguished service, John retired from his beloved

Silver Star Medal of WW2.

Navy in the late 1950s, having attained the rank of full commander.

In civilian life, John managed a California Unemployment Office in Santa Maria; later, he worked as a general foreman for an RV park in Temecula.

John passed away in Tehachapi on February 15, 2015, at the age of 98. He was laid to rest at the Bakersfield National Cemetery in Arvin. He is survived by his son, John H. and Susan Pruden; his daughter, Joan Ferragamo; and by a veritable stable of grandchildren, great-grandchildren, nieces, and nephews.

PART TWO

Korean War Era

CHAPTER 5

Bill Beasley: With the 1st Marine Division at the Chosin Reservoir

Bill was born on October 5, 1930, in the little town of Cody, Nebraska. While still an infant, he and his family moved to the state capital, Lincoln, where Bill grew up and went to school. His father was a baker, his mother worked as (what in those days was called) a "practical nurse," providing 24 hours, seven-day-a-week care to sick and disabled clients.

Bill Beasley, Koto-ri, North Korea Dec. 1950. Photo provided.

Bill got off to a rather rocky start in life. In 1933, his parents separated (they later divorced), and because his mother's job took her out of their home for weeks at a time, Bill was boarded out to family friends. At age seven, his mother somehow managed to place him in a Lutheran orphanage (she paid $15 a month for his board and care), where he lived until he was 12. As Bill wryly put it, "I didn't grow up in a single-parent household, I grew up in a no-parent household."

In junior high, he was boarded out again—this time to a couple who needed a "handyman." Bill earned $5 a month doing chores for the couple. Finally, while still in junior high, he went to live permanently with his mother, who was now working as a checker at a grocery store. (Bill's father, with whom he had little contact, passed away in the late 1940s.)

Bill attended Lincoln High School. "I was a tall, skinny, gangly kid, underweight. So they decided I couldn't stand the rigors of sports. But that never bothered me. I developed an interest in photography and was on the photography club in high school." While in high school, Bill also had a part-time job, working as a "soda jerk" for the local Walgreens Drug Store. He graduated from high school in June 1948.

At that time, Bill decided to join the Navy, but when he went to enlist the Navy recruiting station was closed. Walking home, he happened to pass a Marine Corps recruiting station, which just happened to be open. He stopped and talked with the Marine Corps recruiter, who assured him that the Navy was "out to lunch" (literally it seems!) and that if he joined the Marines, he could leave right away for training in San Diego.

The thought of heading immediately for California appealed to Bill, so he tried to enlist; however, he failed to pass the Marine Corps physical—at 6' 2" and 130 pounds, he was a pound shy of the minimum weight requirement! He was told to go home, stuff himself for a week, and then come back. He did as he was told, and barely made the weight requirement.

Basic training was at the Marine Corps Recruiting Depot in San Diego, and he completed it in September 1948. After further training, Bill hoped to be assigned to a Marine Corps detachment that was deployable aboard Navy combat ships. Yet the Navy was downsizing after World War II, so it didn't have a vessel to put him on. To his dismay, he ended up on a guard detachment at Naval Air Station North Island, Coronado, California.

Nine months later, Private First Class Beasley was assigned to the 1st Marine Division at Camp Pendleton, California. Following a short stint with the 5th Marine Regiment, he was posted to the division's 1st Medical Battalion, for which he was in charge of the barracks that housed the battalion's enlisted personnel. "I had to make sure the barracks were cleaned every morning, that linen was changed once a week, and I issued sheets and blankets to new personnel. It was an easy job. I had lots of time on my hands."

In May 1950, Bill volunteered to serve aboard a light cruiser that had been taken out of "mothballs." Unfortunately, his intent didn't sit well with his 1st Sergeant, who quipped, "If you don't like it here, I can get you a transfer." Bill made the "mistake of answering in the affirmative." He was reassigned to a guard detachment at the Naval ammunition depot in Shoemaker, Arkansas. Not exactly what he'd been looking for!

During the train ride to Arkansas, Bill, and the two Marines accompanying him, stopped to change trains in Dallas-Fort Worth, Texas. While eating lunch at the train depot, they were approached by a man with a newspaper tucked under his arm. The man had paid for their lunch. He opened the newspaper and showed the young Marines the headlines: War had broken out on the Korean peninsula! It was the 25th of June 1950. Upon arrival at the ammunition depot in Shoemaker, Bill and his fellow Marines were greeted by the "officer of the day" in charge of the guard detachment, who bluntly told them, "If I were you guys, I wouldn't unpack my bags!"

Within 30 days, Bill was back at Camp Pendleton, this time assigned to the 1st Marine Division's 1st Marine Regiment, commanded by Lewis B. "Chesty" Puller, who had served with distinction in World War II. As Bill recalled, the regiment was scraped together from personnel

Bill Beasley (in background) with 3.5 inch anti-tank rocket launcher. Photo provided.

all over the country. "Our entire regiment was put together out of bits and pieces of the Marine Corps. We didn't know one another at all." Bill belonged to "Fox" Company of the regiment's 2nd battalion, serving as a gunner for a 3.5 inch anti-tank rocket launcher, a new Army weapon robust enough to handle the Soviet tanks in the North Korean Korean Peoples Army (KPA). Indeed, as Bill noted, the new rocket launcher could "stop a Soviet T-34 in its tracks."

On September 15, 1950, the 1st Marine Division took part in the amphibious assault by U.S. and other United Nations forces at Inchon, South Korea—a bold operation that ended a string of victories by the KPA and was a major strategic success. Bill remembered wading ashore through the mud against weak enemy opposition. Within two weeks, Seoul, the capital of South Korea, was recaptured, and the Marines of the 1st Division temporarily withdrawn to their ships.

A few weeks later, the 1st Marine Division, in another amphibious operation, set down on the eastern coast of North Korea. It advanced inland through rugged and hostile terrain, where the road conditions ranged from poor to non-existent. In late November, in severe winter weather, the Marines were transported by truck to a mountainous region close to the Chosin Reservoir (a man-made lake located deep inside North Korea).

From 27 November to 10 December 1950, the 1st Marine Division fought one of the most desperate (and glorious) battles in Marine Corps history: "Fighting . . . in bitter cold and brutal terrain, men endured severe frostbite, sleepless nights, and total mental and physical exhaustion. Below-zero temperatures, snow-covered mountains, icy roads, and wind-swept cliffs made every skirmish, firefight, and attack a nightmare beyond the men's wildest dreams. . . With tens of thousands of young Americans and Chinese locked in eye-to-eye, hand-to-hand combat in the desolate, freezing mountains surrounding the Chosin Reservoir, the death toll soared. Even men with minor wounds or injuries frequently died. If you stopped moving, you froze. . . None of the men who survived the horrific battle would ever be the same. Today they are called 'The Chosin Few.'" ("The Battle of the Chosin Reservoir," by Ned Forney, October 17, 2018).

The Marines, and supporting U.S. Army, British, and South Korean forces, were vastly outnumbered by the attacking Chinese, whose objective was to isolate and destroy them. Fortunately for Bill, his regiment was the southernmost Marine regiment in the battle, so it didn't bear the brunt of the savage fighting. "We got a little, but we didn't get the worst of it. Our worst enemy was the weather. The winds that blew in from Siberia dropped temperatures, with the wind chill, to 70-75 degrees below zero. The cold weather equipment we had was not designed [for such arctic temperatures]. Engines had to be kept running, or they'd freeze up. Our weapons had to be kept dry of lubrication, or they'd stop working, too. The [rubber] boots we had were totally inadequate. Almost to a man, we had frostbite, frozen feet; men lost their toes and feet. I was fortunate to be cared for by a Navy Corpsman, who helped to save my feet." (Many of the

U.S. Marines in combat at the Chosin Reservoir, late 1950.

Marines who had suffered from the almost indescribable conditions at the Chosin Reservoir would eventually receive 100% disabilities from the Veterans Administration.)

Thanks to effective air support, as well as a specialized "Treadway" bridge that was dropped to span a gaping ravine south of Koto-ri—"I don't remember crossing that bridge, I must have been sleepwalking"—the stalwart Marines of the 1st Marine Division (and supporting forces) were able to avoid potential annihilation by breaking out to the sea. Yet nearly 6000 Americans were dead or missing, and many thousands more wounded.

Bill would see additional combat in the Korean War ("I ate so many cans of pork and beans that to this day I can't stand the sight of them!"), finally returning to the States in September 1951. In late 1952 he married his wife, Nancy, a union that would bring forth three children, six grandchildren, and twelve great-grandchildren. He also realized his dream of becoming a Marine Corps photographer and, in 1966/67, was posted to Vietnam as a combat motion picture cameraman ("even today I have a tough time opening up about Vietnam").

Bill retired from the Marine Corps in 1968, having attained the rank of Gunnery Sergeant (his commendations included a Purple Heart for Korea and seven Air Medals for his service in Vietnam). Bill continued to work as a photographer and in the motion-picture field as a civilian—at the China Lake Naval Weapons Center (15 years) and then at the Dryden Flight Research Center at Edwards Air Force Base. He retired from Federal Civil Service in 1988. Today, he and his wife live a well-deserved peaceful life in California City.

CHAPTER 6

David Rheinhart: Combat with the Navy and the Marine Corps

As always, we begin at the beginning: Dave was born on April 7, 1931, in Indianapolis, Indiana. Sadly, his father "disappeared" when Dave was a small child: "To this day, I still stay in touch with my father's family, but he passed away in his 50s a long time ago." Dave's mother never remarried but went to night school and became a bookkeeper.

David Rheinhart. Photo Provided.

Dave attended public schools in Indianapolis; as a teenager, he attended Arsenal Technical High School (a former Civil War military arsenal), focusing on drafting (several advanced students at the high school worked with the state of Indiana helping to design bridges). He worked his way through high school with the Ziv Steel and Wire Company: "I literally learned the steel business in the four years I worked for them."

After graduation in 1950, he drove his mother to southern California so she could live with other family members. In California, while looking for work, Dave often passed the Navy and Marine Corps recruiting station. One day he thought to himself, "I think I'll join up!" So he did, enlisting in the Navy.

The Navy wanted to send him to Grotin, Connecticut, to be a stores keeper (maintaining clothing, equipment, etc.). "It's a desk job, and I said no way! I joined the Navy to see the world!" So Dave got his wish: he was assigned to the USS Tingey, a Fletcher-class destroyer that was being fitted out for the war in Korea, which had broken out

The USS Tingey Fletcher-Class Destroyer (DD-539) saw active service in both WWII and the Korean War.

in June 1950. Although initially assigned to another job duty, Dave wanted to be a signalman. "I looked up on the signal bridge and saw the men doing what I wanted to do." He "literally begged" the signalman chief quartermaster to take him on and, again, he got his wish. Soon thereafter, the USS Tingey deployed for war, stopping first at Pearl Harbor for gunnery training, then at Midway Island for refueling.

Dave and his destroyer saw their first action at Wonsan Harbor, North

Korea, protecting minesweepers that were clearing minefields (prior to the landing of a Marine regiment there) and lobbing 5-inch shells into the harbor as well. During the winter of 1950/51, the USS Tingey proceeded toward Vladivostok, the largest Russian port on the Pacific Ocean. "I think we were sent there to test the Soviet radar, but I don't know for sure." On another occasion, Dave's destroyer took part in a gun-duel with enemy artillery, which managed to strike both the destroyer in front of and behind the USS Tingey.

Yet Dave's most noteworthy experience at sea during the Korean War was saving the life of one of his shipmates: "It was a very cold and pitch-black night. . . I had to climb a ladder to get up to the torpedo deck. When I arrived on the torpedo deck, I heard a voice pleading, 'please help me, please help me. I'm frozen to the guardrail.'" After assuring the distressed shipmate that he'd return to help him, Dave slipped below deck to grab a bucket of water; then, precariously grasping the bucket in one hand, while the ship rocked in the waves, he struggled his way back up the ladder. Finally back on the torpedo deck, he was able to pour the water on the man's frozen hands to free them. At great risk to his own person, Dave was able to carry his disabled shipmate down the ladder to safety.

In the summer of 1952, Dave volunteered to serve with the Marines on the Korean mainland. He was assigned as a signalman to a coastal reconnaissance company in the 3rd Battalion, 5th Marine Regiment. Here he experienced ground combat. One morning, his unit was attacked by a large contingent of North Korean troops. The Marines called for air support and then watched in awe as a Navy propeller-driven A-1 "Skyraider" fighter-bomber pounded the enemy into submission. "I was shocked by the firepower of the Skyraider," Dave recalled.

Reassigned to the USS Tingey, Dave left Korea in early 1953 (the fighting in Korea ended with an armistice in July 1953). Arriving at the port in Seattle, Washington, Dave and several of his shipmates, all in uniform, had a once-in-a-lifetime experience: As they stood on a street corner, a motorcade of vehicles rolled by—it was President Dwight D. Eisenhower, who had just been elected in November 1952. Eisenhower was in town to give the keynote speech at the annual Governors' convention. Eyeing the young sailors, the president emerged from his vehicle and approached them. "How are they treating you, boys?" he asked. "Just fine, Ike!" was the response. "Well, if they don't, you know where to reach me!"

Shortly thereafter, Dave was discharged from the Navy. Although the Navy had offered to send him to college and officer's candidate school, he demurred ("I probably made the right choice"). Instead, Dave went to work in the aerospace industry, securing good-paying jobs in southern California with General Dynamics (Atlas missile program), the McDonnell Douglas commercial aircraft division, and with North American (B-1 bomber program). At the same time, he worked sporadically, albeit successfully, on a junior college degree.

Dave married in 1978, and both he and his wife, Kathy, attended California State University at Los Angeles, Dave graduating with a Bachelor of Arts in industrial technology, Kathy with a B.A. in speech pathology. In the 1980s, Dave taught technical courses (e.g., basic circuit design) to adult foreign students for the Los Angeles Unified School District (LAUSD). In what was a great honor, he was asked by the city of L.A. to design and oversee the construction of a city time capsule, which is not to be opened until (or about) 2083! He retired from LAUSD in 1987 at age 55.

In the late 1980s, Dave, Kathy, and their two daughters (born in 1983 and 1986) moved to Tehachapi. "We were invited to Tehachapi by an administrator with the LAUSD. He had property there and invited us up. We were so impressed that we discussed buying property, and we did! Then we built our own home."

In retirement, Dave continued to hone a special skill he had worked on, off and on, for decades. In the 1950s, while employed by General Dynamics, he had taken some watercolor painting classes with Bob

Landry (a former art director for the Defense Department) and evinced a remarkable talent as an artist. As years passed, he became a highly-accomplished watercolor painter, "painting everything and anything! I never really took it seriously, but I loved it and got pretty good at it."

After not seeing his mentor, Bob Landry, for many years, Dave had a reunion with Bob at the latter's home in Sante, California. As Dave was departing, Bob said mysteriously, "Goodbye, old friend." Three days later, Landry's wife called to inform him that her husband had passed away. "It shook my soul. I almost fell over."

At the conclusion of the interview, this author asked Dave what military

David Rheinhart and his wife, Kathy, in Tehachapi. Photo Provided.

life had meant to him: “It gave me discipline and a sense of loyalty and honor to God and country. I consider myself a constitutional conservative and I love my country. If I were 70 years younger, I’d probably do it again!”

And Dave, if you were 70 years younger, I have no doubt that the Navy would love to take you back! Kern County salutes you for your service.

CHAPTER 7

Lew Thornton: Defender of Freedom in South Korea

Lew was born in the little town of Crosbyton, Texas, on August 3, 1935. He was the oldest of three boys (the youngest brother dying in a tragic accident in 1939). As Lew recalled: "This was during the Great Depression, and nobody really had anything. My father took any job that he could—he shoveled coal out of a coal car at a railroad station; he drove a truck; he picked grapes and cotton; he did anything to keep our family going."

Lew Thornton. Photo provided.

Despite the desperate efforts of the Roosevelt administration, the Great Depression would not end until the advent of the Second World War. When the United States entered the war in December 1941, it finally eliminated the lingering effects of the depression, dramatically reducing U.S. unemployment; in fact, the massive spending on the war effort doubled economic growth rates, while some 17 million young men went off to war against the Axis powers (Germany, Japan, and Italy).

One of these men was Lew's father, who fought as an Army infantryman in the Pacific theater, where he saw combat and was wounded on the island of Okinawa in 1945. "He didn't like to talk about [his war experiences] too much," Lew said. "He returned home in mid-1945 after he was released from the hospital. All I remember is that he would wake up in the middle of the night, and he'd be in a cold sweat. He told me he was 'reliving what happened overseas.'" Eventually, Lew's father became a truck driver, driving a semi-truck for many years. He would also find employment as a police officer in Los Angeles.

Lew's family had moved to California in the late 1930s. He attended Glendale High School, where he played football and ran track, graduating in June 1954. While in high school, he took an ROTC (Reserve Officer Training Corps) class. "Our high school was one of the first to institute ROTC, the purpose of which was to become

U.S. soldiers stare across the DMZ separating North and South Korea (n.d.).

familiar with the Army and receive credits toward graduation; also, I was determined to follow in my father's footsteps."

Lew entered the Army in September 1954. Basic training took place at Fort Ord, California, and Lew selected armor (tanks) as his specialty. For specialized training to serve in a tank unit, he was dispatched to Fort Knox, Kentucky; thereafter, he was off to Fort Lewis, Washington, and temporarily assigned to the 72nd Tank Battalion (1st Infantry Division).

In December 1954, Private First Class Thornton began the long journey to South Korea, his transport docking at Inchon Bay on Christmas Day. The fighting in Korea, which took the lives of nearly 40,000 American soldiers, had ended on July 27, 1953, with the signing of the Korean Armistice Agreement. The agreement established the Korean Demilitarized Zone (DMZ) to separate North and South Korea, and allowed for the return of prisoners of war; however, no peace treaty was ever signed thus, to this day, the war has not formally ended (and technically continues)

Lew served with the 73rd Heavy Tank Battalion in or near Seoul, the capital of South Korea. He was the commander and gunner of his M-47 "Patton" main battle tank, which boasted a 90mm main armament (with a range of about 1500 yards), two coaxial .30 caliber machine guns and one .50 caliber machine gun. The mission of his tank battalion was to provide armored support for U.S. and South Korean infantry forces along the DMZ while also continuing to train with both U.S. and South Korean forces. "It was still a tense situation," Lew averred, "even though the armistice had been signed. Because the shooting, pot shots really, never stopped. But we never had any fear that a full-blown war would break out again. . . We [were] occupation troops, and through our presence, we were helping to stop another war by preventing North Korea from attacking into South Korea."

When asked what he recalled most about his service in South Korea, Lew responded with a humorous anecdote: "We had something called a 'butt can,' which was a three-pound can into which we threw our cigarette butts, although we weren't allowed to smoke inside our tank. We had two of these cans, and we used one of them to made coffee, the other for cigarette butts!" Let's hope Lew and his crew never mixed up the cans!

Lew was in South Korea for about a year-and-a-half. He then went back to Fort Ord, where he was promoted to staff sergeant. He was mustered out of the Army in 1957. "I've thought about it over the years, wondered what it would have been like if I'd re-enlisted and stayed in the Army. But I decided not to. I was anxious to get back home to be with my family, my brother and parents. My middle brother returned from Germany [where he had served in the Army] about the same time I returned from South Korea."

Back home, Lew found employment at the same firm for which his father worked as a truck driver (the company made concrete) and worked there for several years. He got married in 1960, the marriage bringing forth a son and a daughter (he would remarry years later). In 1961, again following in his father's footsteps, he became a police officer in Glendale. He also found time to go to college, earning an undergraduate degree in police science from California State University Los Angeles in the early 1970s.

Lew worked with the Glendale Police Department for 23 years, ending his career flying a helicopter. "I loved [being a police officer]. I loved every second of it. First of all, I joined the police department because I wanted to get out and help the public, to curtail crime. Also, my dad had been a police officer in Los Angeles." Following his retirement from the police force in 1985, Lew worked security with a government contractor for the U.S. Air Force at Air Force Plant 42 (Palmdale, California) for 18 years, retiring from this position in 2003.

This author asked Lew how he ended up in Tehachapi: "Susan [his second wife] and I liked to get out and travel a bit. We decided to go up to Tehachapi because we saw something about a property for sale. We loved Tehachapi, bought a property in late 1985, had a contractor design and build a house, and have been here ever since."

In January 2019, Lew joined the Bear Valley Springs Veterans Association, with which he serves as part of the honor guard. "We conduct parades and also participate in funerals at the Bakersfield Veterans Memorial Cemetery. We also support our community. Recently we purchased a flag pole and mounted it in a nice ceremony at a local grade school. We go to Tehachapi High School every year to attend a ceremony in the gymnasium to honor our military."

In April 2020, Lew was whisked away to Washington D.C. (along with two dozen other veterans and their chaperones, one for each veteran), by Honor Flight Kern County. He and his fellow veterans were delighted to visit the moving memorials for World War II, the Korean and Vietnam Wars, as well as other historic sights in the capitol. Lew was most grateful for the experience. "I treasured every minute of it," he said.

Lew Thornton—We treasure you, your father, and your brother for your selfless service to our great country in both war and peace!

PART THREE

Vietnam War Era

CHAPTER 8

Jed Hannan:
Aboard the Essex-Class Carrier USS Bon Homme Richard

U.S. Navy veteran Jed Hannan was born in Jacksonville, Florida, in November 1943; this, of course, was in the middle of World War II, and Jed's father was an aviation machinist's mate in the Navy at Jacksonville Naval Air Station (NAS), where he rebuilt engines on PBY flying boats.

Raised in New Jersey and the oldest of six children, Jed graduated from high school in June 1961. The day after graduation, he and a friend began a most ambitious road trip: inspired by President John F. Kennedy, and wanting to show that "American youth aren't soft," they rode their bicycles from New Jersey to Sacramento,

California! About halfway through their journey, however, they split up in Kansas City, and Jed rode the second half of the route by himself. The road trip took six weeks. The two boys then hooked up again and toured much of California on their bicycles.

Jed then flew back to New Jersey, where he worked as a shipping clerk for a short time. In the fall of 1962, he returned to California, this time driving his 1954 Chevrolet to Sacramento, where he lived with a friend. He got a part-time job at a gas station, making $1.25 an hour. Seeing no future pumping gas, Jed joined the Navy in January 1963 and went to boot camp in San Diego. In boot camp, Jed was placed in a class of recruits that was struggling with, as Jed described it, "the academic-type stuff." Because Jed had done well in high school (he had elected not to go to college), he asked his chief petty officer if he could help to tutor these recruits; the chief petty officer ("the toughest guy in our group; nobody gave him any crap!") readily agreed. Jed assisted the recruits in studying the various instructional and training manuals; in fact, he was so successful that his class received an award for scoring the highest in the academic portion of the training.

After a short period of leave, Jed, following in his father's footsteps, was sent to Jacksonville NAS. Here he took basic aviation ordnance training, graduating in the summer of 1963 with the rank of E2 Seaman, a junior enlisted rank. In September 1963, Jed was assigned to Lemoore NAS, near Fresno; here, he took a number of training courses, and, in January 1964, became an "Aviation Ordnance Man 3rd Class" (equivalent to a Private First Class in the U.S. Army). He was then assigned to Attack Squadron 196, equipped with 12 Douglas A-1 "Skyraider" single-seat attack aircraft. The Skyraider had entered military service shortly after World War II, becoming the backbone of the Navy's aircraft carrier and Marine Corps' strike sorties in the Korean War (1950-53). As an aviation ordnance specialist, Jed's mission was the maintain the bomb racks and 20mm aircraft cannon on the A-1 aircraft.

In February 1964, Jed's squadron was transferred to the naval base

Jed Hannan holding a 100lb. Bomb. Photo provided.

in San Diego and assigned to the USS Bon Homme Richard (CVA 31), an Essex Class aircraft carrier built in 1944 that had seen service in the Pacific late in World War II. The Bon Homme Richard soon headed out for Hawaii and back into the Pacific region; Jed's training at this time included loading live bombs and helping to load (unarmed) nuclear weapons onto the Skyraiders. Along with the typical training maneuvers, ports of call included the Philippines (Subic Bay Naval Base), Hong Kong ("liberty call"), and naval bases in southern Japan. On one occasion, Jed took part in a bus tour to Nagasaki, where the second atom bomb had been dropped on August 9, 1945; there, he visited the museum at "ground zero," an experience he found "very sobering, seeing all the photos, as well as some buildings that have never been rebuilt; they were left as memorials."

The Bon Homme Richard was then dispatched on a goodwill voyage, entering the Indian Ocean on April 4, 1964, as part of the "Concord Squadron," composed of the carrier, several destroyers, and the fleet oiler. The cruise lasted six weeks and took the Bon Homme Richard near Iran, the Arabian Peninsula, and then along the African coast and into many ports for goodwill visits.

Yet Jed, his aircraft attack squadron, and the Bon Homme Richard were soon taking part in more serious ventures, for the Vietnam War was heating up. By the summer of 1964, the Bon Homme Richard was on a training mission in the Gulf of Tonkin, off the coast of North Vietnam. On August 2nd, about 9:00 p.m., general quarters were sounded (i.e., man your battle stations!). Jed immediately went to his aviation ordnance shop, where the men played cards, read books, and, of course, wondered what was up. After about 30 minutes, the public address system crackled: "Good evening men, this is the captain

Photograph from 1960s revealing the power and strength of the aircraft carrier USS Bon Homme Richard (CVA 31).

speaking. North Vietnamese torpedo boats have attacked the destroyer USS Maddox. They have fired torpedoes as an act of war. I repeat, this is not a drill!" Jed and his fellow sailors were stunned: "We weren't too happy about it. We knew we weren't very far from Communist China and that they had long-range bombers and missiles." Late that night, planes were loaded with fuel and bombs and launched into the gulf. Eventually, Jed asked one of the returning pilots, "What happened out there?" His riposte: "Son, we're at war."

From August to November 1964, the fighters and attack aircraft aboard the Bon Homme Richard flew almost daily combat missions in support of Allied forces in South Vietnam. In his role as ordnance specialist, Jed loaded bombs and napalm onto his squadron's A-1 Skyraiders, and armed and maintained their 20mm cannon.

In December, Jed took a month of well-earned leave back in New Jersey. While there, he met his future wife and was married in February 1965; together, they drove back to Lemoore Naval Air Station in California. From April 1965 to January 1966, Jed and his carrier were again seeing service off the coast of Vietnam. As Jed recalled, he and the other ordnance specialists were "on duty 18 hours a day," loading bombs or ammunition onto the planes and doing maintenance. The pace of work was exhausting, even for young men in great physical shape, resulting in a mishap still etched in Jed's mind:

"We were de-arming the cannon, removing the rounds that hadn't been fired on the Skyraiders. The [other] ordnance specialist was so tired he had neglected to de-arm the shells out of the last gun on one of the A-1s [each aircraft had four 20mm cannon]. He was in the cockpit; I was on the deck when it happened. He pulled the trigger—the gun was supposed to be empty—to close the gun bolts to keep them from rusting, for they could rust in a matter of hours from the saltwater. Well, all hell broke loose. About 20 rounds were fired off! They hit the mast of the ship, cutting some of the carrier's communication cables."

Fortunately, there were no casualties. An inquiry followed, with the captain hearing the evidence. The captain, however, acutely aware that the men had been worked to the point of exhaustion for days on end, elected to not take action against Jed or his workmate. "It's amusing now," Jed recalled, "but it was terrifying when it happened."

Jed left the Navy in April 1966 when his enlistment expired. In the decades that followed, living in Glendale, California, with his wife and growing family (four daughters), he worked mainly as a salesman, selling home furnishings and textile products to department and specialty stores. He retired in 2012. Before retiring, however, Jed and his family moved to Tehachapi in 2002 ("to get out of the rat race in Los Angeles"), where one of his daughters and her family reside.

Finally, Jed has a message for young people everywhere who might be considering a career in the military: "The military is an outstanding experience to help young people. The military gives you a good foundation in life; a way to serve your country. We need the military. We need to be strong. We need to protect our freedoms."

Thank you for your service, Jed! Kern County and America salute you!

CHAPTER 9

Thomas Morris (1):
Air Force Mechanic, Marine Corps Crew Chief

Tom Morris was born on March 13, 1943, in a blackout in the middle of World War II. As he told this author, "Everything was blacked out due to the military aircraft companies [Douglas, North American Aviation, etc.] and naval ports in the area. I should add that I was the first male baby born at St. John's Hospital in Santa Monica." Tom's mother was a stay-at-home mom who had moved to California in the late 1930s from Rapid City, South Dakota, where she had been chosen "Miss Rapid City." "She was a very beautiful woman."

Tom's father worked as an engineer for North American, and "was probably the only person who ever sat in all of Jimmy Doolittle's B-25B bombers," which conducted the raid over Japan in April 1942 that electrified an American nation desperate for a military success over Japan in the early months after Pearl Harbor. Tom's father went on to become a production manager for the famous P-51 "Mustang" fighter (also built by North American), until drafted into the Navy in late 1944. In the Navy, he soon contracted scarlet fever and was sent to a Navy hospital in San Diego; he survived the serious disease, but the sailors in the beds on either side of him did not. Recovering and back in training, he was assigned to the destroyer USS Storms (DD 780), but was soon in the hospital again—this time with a double hernia! As a result, he was unable to ship out with his vessel, an act of Fortuna that most likely saved his life: The destroyer was struck by a kamikaze aircraft, killing 21 and wounding 15; the kamikaze had hit precisely where his battle station was located (he had been trained as a loader on a 40mm Bofors anti-aircraft gun crew).

Tom went to Arcadia High School in the San Gabriel Valley, where he met "The Loop Newspaper's" future owner, Claudia Needham (now Needham-Baker). She became Tom's first girlfriend. In high school, he participated in basketball, track, tennis, and football (the latter being his main sport), graduating in June 1961.

After graduation, Tom got a job at the local Broadway Department Store, part of a major chain at that time. He worked in the store's distribution center in Los Angeles, driving to work in a 1942 Ford, a vehicle that was quite rare because Ford had by then transitioned to making tanks for the war effort (instead of civilian cars and trucks). The department store had a nasty habit of terminating employees at 90 days, so it didn't have to offer raises. Tom was aware of this and, thus, convinced that the same unhappy fate awaited him upon reaching the 90-day threshold. So what did he do? He enlisted in the Air Force in February 1962, totally unaware that management had been grooming him for a better position! Indeed, he was actually offered a raise and a technical position in the printing department but, alas, Tom, like Caesar before him, had already crossed the Rubicon!

Tom was soon on a train winding its way toward Lackland AFB, Texas, for basic training. Also aboard the train was a clutch of newly-minted Marines, whom Tom encountered in the dining car. As Tom remembered it: "One of the Marines must have been misbehaving, because their drill instructor stood up and barked at him, 'watch that mouth of yours, or I'll crack it open!' I thought to myself: 'If this is how we're going to be treated in the military, what have I done?' I was wishing I was with my three buddies who'd gone off to college."

Tom's train pulled in to Lackland about 4.00 in the morning. A good California boy, he was clad only in Bermuda shorts and a Hawaiian shirt, oblivious to the fact that the weather in Texas was freezing cold! He and the other recruits were "greeted" at the bus that was to take them on to the base by their drill instructor, who had a warm and cuddly message for the tired and bleary-eyed recruits: "My name is Sergeant Ducho, and you're all gonna hate the day you met me!" But Tom made it through boot camp with flying colors; in fact, he was selected among the recruits as one of the squad leaders for basic training. "It was kind of scary, but we all managed to get through it."

Tom completed basic in April 1962. Then it was on to technical school at Shepherd AFB, Texas, for training as a reciprocating engine (i.e., piston engine) aircraft mechanic. In September 1962, Airman 3rd Class Morris was sent to Wheelus Air Base (Tripoli, Libya) on an 18-month assignment. Tension and excitement were not long coming, as the base soon found itself on red alert during the Cuban Missile Crisis of October 1962. "Our fighter aircraft at the base were outfitted with ordnance for a possible war with the Soviet Union."

From June to September 1963, he went TDY to Vietnam, where he was assigned to an air base in Saigon and worked as a mechanic on AC-47 gunship engines. On the final day of his TDY—and this at a time when few Americans were even aware of Vietnam and the conflict slowing simmering there—while flying into Saigon on final approach after an engine check, Tom was shot in the foot by Viet Cong small-arms fire (a shell had penetrated the bottom of the fuselage and his boot). Although he hardly felt the wound, he observed blood oozing onto the floor and realized he'd been shot. During this first sojourn to Vietnam, Tom was awarded the Purple Heart and the Bronze Star for his service. As he explained, "I also took part in a couple of missions that I really can't talk about."

Tom Morris next to a Marine Corps H-34D helicopter. Photo provided.

Returning to Wheelus AB, Airman 1st Class Morris (he had been promoted while in Vietnam) was detailed to the Marine Corps to do helicopter maintenance. The Marines had two Sikorsky, multi-purpose, piston-driven, H-34 helicopters at Wheelus; the problem was, however, they had no mechanics to work on the engines. Eventually, Tom was approached by a Marine Corps colonel with a rather unique proposition: Would he consider transferring to the Corps? The colonel sweetened the deal by assuring Tom he would be promoted to E-5 in both the Marine Corps (i.e., sergeant) and the Air Force (staff sergeant). Tom agreed to the transfer. (Note: despite the transfer, he was still assigned to the USAF for administrative purposes).

In March 1964, the Marines sent Tom to San Diego for additional training, including combat training. In May, he moved on to Edwards AFB, where he was assigned to a helicopter squadron as a reciprocating engine mechanic. He recalled: "This was a most exciting time at Edwards. I saw the first landing of the XB-70 "Valkyrie" bomber. There was also the X-15 hypersonic rocket-powered aircraft, and all kinds of other experimental planes." Soon, however, the Marines introduced the CH-46 "Sea Knight" helicopter with two jet engines. So, once again, Sergeant Morris was off to school—this time in Long Beach to learn how to work on the CH-46's engines.

In September 1964, Tom began a standard one-year tour in Vietnam, stationed at Na Trang Air Base as part of the 1st Marine Division. "As far as I know, we were the first Marines to have boots on the ground in Vietnam. It was pretty clandestine. We performed rescue, mercy and hygiene missions. We went by helicopter into villages with the doctors. We taught the villagers proper childbirth, we deloused them, cleaned them up, provided them with soap and shampoo. We took seriously ill people into the base at Na Trang for surgery." Tom would

C-123 Transport landing at a base in South Vietnam.

fly 54 of these missions during his second posting to Vietnam.

At Na Trang, he worked on C-123 transports, modified with spray tanks to discharge "Agent Orange" (a herbicide and defoliant chemical) in missions designed to deprive the Viet Cong of food and cover as part of Operation "Ranch Hand," the U.S. military's chemical warfare program in Vietnam that lasted from 1962 to 1971. "We had no idea at the time how lethal Agent Orange was, and it had a horrible smell," Tom explained. "Many of the men I worked with, or crew members of those C-123s, have since passed away from cancer, perhaps due to exposure to Agent Orange. Our government in recent years has finally acknowledged the lethal problems caused by exposure to it."

About a month into his tour, Tom, while returning from a mission, looked down from his Marine Corps helicopter to see smoke billowing up out of the hotel where he and his men were billeted: Viet Cong guerillas had destroyed the hotel with explosive charges. "This was when I realized that we really couldn't tell friend from foe. I saw some terrible things that happened to the Vietnamese people. The South Vietnamese Army could be quite cruel to anyone they suspected of being an enemy or supporting the enemy."

Then came May 28, 1965—"that horrible day" as Tom described it. (To be continued in the following chapter.)

CHAPTER 10

Thomas Morris (2): May 28, 1965—That Horrible and Unforgettable Day

An urgent call came in from a Navy fighter pilot whose plane had been struck by enemy fire. The pilot had ejected and gone down in enemy-held territory. Tom and his search and rescue team immediately boarded their helicopter and dashed off toward the coordinates provided by the pilot. Soon the helicopter was hovering over him. Tom, in addition to being the crew chief and left-door gunner, was also the hoist operator. He lowered the hoist, but the downed pilot was unable to grasp it (the Navy pilot, a lieutenant, had been badly injured ejecting from his plane; in fact, both his shoulders had been crushed and he was completely incapacitated). We'll let Tom take it from here:

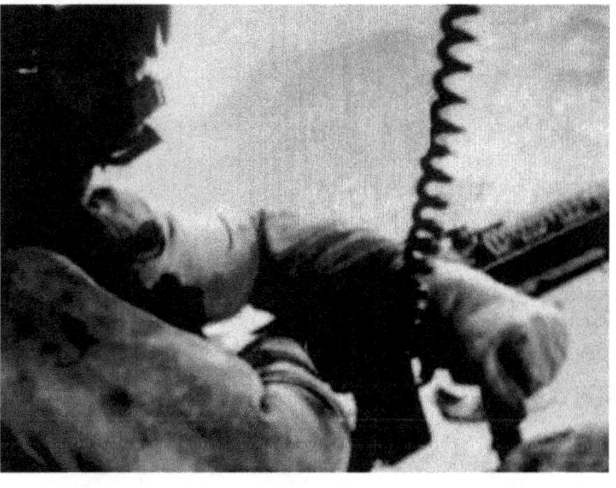

Taking wounded to a field hospital at Da Nang. "I remember it was a clear day just before monsoon season, in April 1965." Photo by Stars & Stripes.

"Because he couldn't grab hold of the hoist, I had to go down and get him. The crew lowered me down. No sooner was I on the ground than I heard a blast—the entire front rotor was blown off the helicopter, and it went straight down. All I heard were screams. It was merciful that all my crew members were killed almost instantly. I was only slightly injured in the blast.

"Then two Viet Cong came round the corner, lugging a knee-operated mortar, which they had used to take down the helicopter. They were laughing. I shot them both dead with my M-14 rifle. I reached the downed pilot just as it was getting dark. We were very close to a village that was crawling with VC. The villagers were swarming the area, trying to find us; they were armed with knives, spears, and guns. I had to shoot many of them.

"Of course, we had to try and stay hidden from the villagers, so I grabbed the pilot by his collar and kept schlepping him around to new locations. Eventually, I got shot in the head, but I was saved by my helmet, which was sturdier than a typical helmet because it was fitted with some communications gear. The shot, however, grazed my forehead, which bled profusely. At times I could hardly see as my eyes were covered in blood. During the course of the night, I finally got the lieutenant under a pepper tree, and things seemed to be quieting down. By now, I had used up all ammunition for my .357 Magnum service revolver, my M-14 rifle, and the pilot's .45 caliber 1911 pistol.

"Suddenly, I was charged by someone with a sword! He lunged at me, caught me on the side of my flight suit and ribcage, pinning me to a tree. As he struggled to pull his sword out of the tree, I managed, despite my loss of blood, to reach down and grab my Ka-Bar knife from my leg scabbard and, in the flickering moonlight, which enabled me to make out my attacker, I thrust my knife up under his jaw, and it exited one of his eyes. That's all I remember."

Tom and the Navy pilot were rescued by an Air Force air rescue unit and immediately brought to the military hospital at Clark Air Base in the Philippines. Tom had been wounded a ghastly total of 13 times and nearly lost an arm. He spent four months recovering at Clark AB, and then was sent to Hawaii for two more months of rehabilitation. For his many acts of heroism on that "horrible day," Tom received a Purple Heart and the Silver Star.

The Navy pilot—Marc Lender, from a distinguished Jewish family on the east coast (founders of the Lender's Bagel Company)—recovered and made it home. "So all of sudden," Tom recalled, "I had a Jewish mother! Every Christmas, I would get a card from her saying, 'you saved my son!'" Tom and Marc became good friends, and remain so to his very day.

In December 1965, Tom's duty with the Marine Corps came to an end. Back on regular duty with the Air Force, he became an instructor

The prestigious Navy Cross. After the Medal of Honor, it is the highest award a member of the United States Navy, U.S. Marines, or U.S. Coast Guard may earn.

at Edwards Air Force Base, training helicopter gunners. However, he was only on Air Force active duty for about 45 days, and was mustered out of the service in January 1966.

Yet in the spirit of the inimitable Paul Harvey, there's still more to Tom's remarkable story. In 1967, he was honored at a ceremony at the Marine Barracks in San Diego. Vice-President Hubert Humphrey personally presented him with the Navy Cross (an upgrade of the original Silver Star) and two artifacts that had been recovered from the battle area—the sword with which he had been stabbed, and his .357 Magnum service revolver. It was only during this unique event that Tom finally learned he had killed 14 of the enemy that day. (Note: Tom's military records concerning the events of May 28, 1965, are sealed until 2041: "Long after I'm gone, many books will be written about President Johnson, Secretary of Defense [Robert] McNamara, and General Alexander Haig. Many people died on missions no one will ever know about.")

Meanwhile, after leaving the military, Tom used his G.I. Bill benefits to go back to school, earning an AA degree in accounting at Orange Coast College, in Costa Mesa, followed by a BA degree from UCLA in 1971, also in accounting. In 1969, Tom had tied the knot with Barbara, their marriage bringing forth a girl in 1970 and a boy in 1976.

In the late 1960s and into the mid-1970s, Tom, along with a buddy who was also a Vietnam veteran, started and ran two successful entrepreneurial ventures—a retail outfit in Anaheim that installed eight-track stereo systems in automobiles (based on a business of his father's); and a backpacking store with a total capital investment of just $6000. "We sold the best backpacking equipment one could buy, all German or Swiss made; in 1976, we were bought out by a Big-5 sporting goods store," he said.

Yet Tom's primary "meal ticket" was, as one might suspect, in the accounting field. In 1976, Tom, Barbara, and the children moved to

Petaluma in Northern California, where he went to work for the big accounting firm, Price Waterhouse. Several years later (1979), Tom was again back to school, this time securing an MA in accounting from UC Berkeley.

Tom then rejoined Price Waterhouse in Petaluma but, by the end of 1980, had opened up his own accounting firm in Santa Rosa. The years went by, and Tom built on his successful career as a CPA. Then, in 1993, his mother suffered a serious stroke; in response, he retired from his firm and moved down to La Quinta (near Palm Springs) to care for her. In 2009, tragedy struck again, with Tom's wife, Barbara, passing away.

Following the death of his mother in 2010, Tom decided to go back to work. "I got bored being retired, so I went to work for the Department of Homeland Security in Port Hueneme, one of the largest deep-water ports on the west coast. For DHS, we secured ships coming into port for any contraband and drove exotic cars [e.g., Austin Martins, Maseratis, Mercedes] to a staging point on the military base at Port Hueneme. And I'm still doing this! Although now I'm on furlough due to the pandemic. I'm hoping to be back at work soon."

Sergeant Morris: For more than four decades, this author has interviewed and corresponded with hundreds of veterans from WWII to the recent conflicts in Afghanistan and Iraq; and yet, your description of the events of May 28, 1965, is one of the most harrowing "profiles in courage" I have ever encountered. Kern County and America salute you!

CHAPTER 11

Daryl M. Black: By Train, Ship, or Plane, He got it to its Destination!

Born in Independence, Iowa on June 20, 1934, Daryl Black was the oldest of three children in his family. As he fondly recalled, "Mom always said I was born first so I could take care of [my parents'] two younger daughters." Daryl's father was a machinist with John Deere. In 1951, the family moved to Waterloo, Iowa, where he completed high school, graduating in 1953. He had played football in high school and, growing up with a fascination for trains like so many young boys, had also found employment at the railroad in Waterloo as a switchman. As Daryl noted, this was quite a responsibility for a teenager, "but I was well supervised." Daryl did not go to college, but in October 1953, he took on an even greater responsibility, getting married to his high school sweetheart, Jackie, whom he had known since kindergarten

Continuing to work as a railroad switchman after high school, yet having no seniority and being aware he'd most likely be drafted into the military, he decided to enlist in the Army in June 1954. His decision to enlist in the Army was influenced, in part, by a history of family members serving in the Army over the years.

Daryl Black in Vietnam. Photo provided.

After completing basic training at Fort Bliss, Texas, and (due to his earlier experience as a railroad switchman) a brief stint at transportation school at Fort Eustis, Virginia, Daryl began a nearly 20-year military career in transportation services that would take him over much of the world. Among his initial assignments were: Bremerhaven, Germany (1955/56), where he processed U.S. military personnel coming in and out of the port (he made Private First Class during this first major assignment); Fort Ord, California (1958/60), where he worked on flight scheduling; La Rochelle, France (1960/63), where he supervised a transportation warehouse (the warehouse was a WW2 German Navy torpedo storage bunker, with eight-foot thick ceilings and eight- to 10-foot thick walls); and Fort Irwin, California (1963/65), where he supervised the off-loading of tracked vehicles (including tanks, tracked howitzers and armored personnel carriers) from the railroad and shepherded them to Fort Irwin, where units were building up for Vietnam.

These first 10 years of Daryl's military career had brought more than a few highlights. In France, he had observed filming of Darryl F. Zanuck's classic war movie, *The Longest Day*, much of which was shot just off the coast of La Rochelle on an island that still had many intact

German WW2 bunkers. (Daryl would spend two months shipping military equipment back to Germany, including vehicles and tents used by Zanuck for the movie.) Yet the most noteworthy highlights of this period were the births of his and Jackie's three daughters in 1957,

The AC-47 gunship boasted a trio of GAU-2/M134 miniguns that collectively could unload 6000 rounds per minute. To maximize effectiveness and minimize risk, the gunships typically operated at night.

1959, and 1963. (Jackie had joined Daryl in Germany in 1955, after completing her training as a registered nurse.)

In December 1965, Daryl left Fort Irwin and arrived in Vietnam in January 1966 (his family was now in Barstow). While in Vietnam, Daryl took part in port operations at Na Trang, his mission activities embracing the construction of port infrastructure, including a pier, and the in-processing of U.S. troop transports. About his Vietnam experience, he said: "I don't even like to talk about it now, but we lost some people" to Viet Cong guerilla activities. While he did not take part in any combat at Na Trang, he did see the mighty AC-47 gunships—called "Puff the Magic Dragon" in the idiom of the Vietnam soldier—in action not far from his base; they were truly a sight to behold.

Daryl returned to Fort Irwin in January 1967. In December, Daryl, his wife, and three daughters left California for another adventure—this time in Cadiz, Spain, where Daryl was assigned to the U.S. Army Transportation Terminal Unit there. "This was strictly nothing but port operations, loading and unloading cargo for the USAF and the Navy. It was a great [three year] assignment, a small operation, and everyone enjoyed it; everyone had their family with them," he said.

Daryl, Jackie, and their children returned to the States in December 1970, and, after getting his family situated in southern California, the peripatetic Army veteran was off to South Korea in January 1971. Again, his mission was to fulfill military transportation requirements, in this case, including requirements for various missile sites. Back in the U.S. by the beginning of 1972, he completed one more assignment (Army sub-port in Long Beach-San Pedro area) before retiring from the Army on June 30, 1974, with the rank of E-7 (Sergeant First Class).

Looking back, Daryl recalled: "I had not planned on staying in the military when I went in, but when I realized opportunities with the civilian railroad were not what I had hoped for, I decided to stay in. I had some good assignments, and I was very happy to have my family with me. We spent 10 years together in Europe."

Daryl and his family remained in Orange County after his retirement (they had moved to El Toro in 1972 after Daryl returned from South Korea). The former high school railroad switchman and Army transportation veteran worked in civilian life as a traffic manager and warehouse supervisor for a consumer hardware company. He retired in 1986.

Daryl and Jackie left El Toro for Tehachapi in late 1993. Their oldest daughter and her family had moved to Tehachapi several years before, which, no doubt, influenced their decision to make the move. Moreover, in 1964/65, Daryl had come through Tehachapi—and been impressed with what he saw—while moving troops from Fort Irwin to the Oakland Army Terminal. He and Jackie love the "easier way of life" here and being close to family.

We salute Daryl Black, his wife, Jackie, and their three daughters for the many sacrifices they made serving our great country!

CHAPTER 12

Ron Rich: .50 Caliber Machine Gunner in Task Force 117

Ron was born in Wichita, Kansas, on September 6, 1947. His father, just out of the service—he had fought with the Army in the Pacific Theater, at one time becoming trapped behind Japanese lines for six months until being rescued—was going to school in Wichita for the Boeing Aircraft Company, for which he would work as a machinist for several years. As a young boy, Ron moved back and forth between Wichita and the little town of Norwood, Missouri, where his family owned a dairy farm. Ron's mother was a "farmer's wife. She stood about 4' 9" tall but was a tough little cookie. She was my rock. I could always depend on her. She was always reading her bible; believed in the Lord same as I do now,"

Ron Rich. Photo provided.

he noted fondly.

Between the ages of seven and 12, Ron received quite an introduction to hard work on the family farm. His day began at 3.30 in the morning. His many responsibilities included milking cows (lots of them!), feeding hogs, and driving a tractor. "I was strong as a bull ox! When I was just nine years old, I was lifting 75 lb. bales of hay. I had to walk a mile to get the bus to school."

In the late 1950s, the Rich family pulled up stakes and moved to Bakersfield, where Mr. Rich had taken a job with Hopper's Machine Shop, making casings for the military's nuclear bombs through the early 1960s. In Bakersfield, Rich attended East Bakersfield High School for a short time and then transferred to North High School. In high school, Ron competed in track and cross-country while also taking part in the men's choir. "I had a hard time catching up [academically] in school," he said. "Because the education levels in Missouri and California were quite different. But I was into English and really loved literature."

In his senior year at North High, Ron joined the Navy Reserves and, in 1964, went to boot camp in San Diego during his Christmas vacation. He graduated from high school in 1965. Two months later, he was on a ship, heading for Vietnam. "I was on the transport USS Okanogan, and we were bringing some 1200 Marines and all their gear and supplies to Vietnam. It was a quick trip, and we were soon back in the states."

Not long thereafter, Ron learned that the Navy was seeking volunteers—for what, he wasn't quite sure, but he elected to volunteer anyway. After 30-days leave, he reported to the big Naval base at Mare Island (close to Vallejo, California). Here, he found out that the Navy was developing a new tactical concept—that of the Mobile Riverine Force (MRF), which would become one of the few "joint" units of the Vietnam War, with Army infantry, artillery and other commands working closely together with small Navy riverine craft to help thwart

Communist aggression.

As a result, Ron was assigned to a heavily modified World War II landing craft, now outfitted with weapons and reinforced with armor plating to enhance survivability. His vessel, for which Ron served as the starboard .50 caliber machine gunner, was part of MRF's Task Force 117 (TF 117). Specifically, the riverine craft of the task force were to cooperate with the Army's 9th Infantry Division—patrolling inland waterways, transporting the Army units to combat zones, and supporting them with weapons that, in addition to heavy machine guns and anti-aircraft guns (for use against ground targets), included flamethrowers ("we called them 'Zippo,' like the cigarette lighter") and giant water pumps to flood enemy bunkers on the banks of rivers.

However, before his unit (Task Force 117, Division 111) was dispatched to Vietnam, it trained on the sloughs near Travis AFB, California, to prepare for the waterways of Vietnam. "We named our boat the 'Swamp Fox,' after the Disney movie," Ron said. "We were the birth of the maritime expeditionary security forces."

Patrolling inland waterways of South Vietnam. Photo provided.

In February 1967, Ron's unit arrived at Dong Tam Naval Base, Vietnam. In the months that followed, he would participate in dozens of missions along the circuitous, jungle-like, and often lethal waterways of the Mekong Delta. One of the "worst missions" took place in April 1967—the "Battle of Snoopy's Nose" (so-called due to the unusual shape of the river, a small tributary of the Song River). "We got caught in terrible enemy fire. We lost some guys, lost some boats. I lost two of my best friends. But we accomplished our mission and destroyed the enemy."

Yet the costly mission of April 1967 was hardly unique for Ron and his mobile riverine warriors. As he put it, "We got into some really nasty stuff. In many operations, TF 117 suffered serious losses in boats and crews. In some operations, we really got 'whacked.' But we posed a serious problem for the enemy. We cut off his waterways, cleaned up the villages, cut off his movements. We'd track them, drop off the 9th Division infantry, who would make a big sweep and take out the enemy. We'd cut'em off at the water."

Ron's deployment with Task Force 117 ended in December 1967. But the task force continued its operations in Vietnam for several more years, despite an extremely high casualty rate; in fact, 3000 men of TF 117 (both Navy sailors and soldiers of the 9th Infantry Division) never returned home. The task force's terrible sacrifice, its extraordinary record of courage and perseverance, is reflected in the fact that it had more Medal of Honor recipients (11) than any other formation (Army, Navy, Air Force, Marines) in the Vietnam War.

As for Ron, he was only wounded once. "It was just a scratch, so I didn't put in for a Purple Heart." For his service in the task force, he garnered the Navy's Meritorious Achievement Medal with a Combat "V" for Valor, the Combat Action Ribbon, and the Navy Reserve Meritorious Achievement Medal with a Combat "V" for Valor (Note: Ron was on active duty in the Navy Reserve during this time.)

Returning to civilian life in 1968 (Ron remained in the Navy Reserve, but had completed his two-year service commitment), he found it difficult to readjust. "They didn't want me. I was rejected big time. I was a Vietnam veteran. I was a 'baby killer.'" By 1972, Ron had a serious decision to make—either "reup" in the reserve, join the regular Navy, or leave the military altogether. Because of his ongoing estrangement from the civilian world, and because "the Navy was where I felt safe," he decided to enlist in the regular Navy.

In the years that followed, the American withdrawal from Vietnam was underway and, by early 1975, was coming to a sad, confusing, and chaotic end. In April 1975, Ron was again back in Vietnam, this time taking part in Operation Eagle Pull—an effort to exfiltrate American personnel from the U.S. Embassy in Saigon and to save Vietnamese refugees terrified of being left behind and at the mercy of Viet Cong or regular North Vietnamese forces. "It was a scary time," Ron remembered. "Refugees were hanging off the tops of ships. I don't know how those ships even stayed afloat. These people were desperate to get out." Ron and his boat crew helped to rescue hundreds of refugees from certain death had they been left behind. "God put me there for a purpose. I saw all sides of humanity. I saw desperation like I'd never seen before."

When Ron returned to the states, "PTSD finally caught up with me. I finally cracked." Following an incident involving Ron and a young and inexperienced senior officer, he was sent to a Navy hospital for psychiatric care. He remained at the hospital for two months yet, fortunately, the care he received there was helpful to him. To this day, however, as Ron forthrightly admitted, he still struggles from time to time with PTSD.

Ron left the Navy in the late 1970s, having attained the rank of Petty Officer, 2nd Class. In the decades that ensued, he worked many different jobs, for example, as an environmental systems technician with the FAA in Bakersfield. He retired in the late 1980s as an assistant scientist in a biology laboratory for Kent Sea Farms, a contractor employed by the Diablo nuclear power plant in San Luis Obispo County.

As our interview neared its end, Ron intimated to this author that he had not only left Vietnam with serious PTSD issues but that he had also suffered grievous exposure to the chemical defoliant Agent Orange. “They’d come through and spray down the [Mekong] delta, and a week later, there wouldn’t be a leaf left!” In fact, he was first diagnosed with problems most likely attributable to Agent Orange while still in the Navy—“basal cells, they would show up as little red sores, and then they’d get bigger; [many years later] they finally got into my jaw and attacked my jaw bone. Still, the government won’t recognize it as having to do with Agent Orange.”

In 2013, Ron lost a lung. He is now on 100% disability from PTSD

Ron Rich and his wife, Glenda. Photo provided.

and other health issues most likely related to Agent Orange. Yet despite his trials, he remains optimistic and has not lost his sense of humor: "I'm OK. I'm alive, but I don't have any teeth because I don't have a jawbone, so I can't bite anybody. But I'm still pretty cute!"

Giving him added strength and purpose is his wife, Glenda, whom he married in 2015 (Ron had three male children from two previous marriages). "She's been my rock and my support. She and the Lord are what keep me going."

CHAPTER 13

Alex Athans: "B" Battery, Ist Battalion, 83rd Artillery

Alex was born in Stoughton, Wisconsin, just months before the United States entered World War II. He and his eight siblings (Alex was No. 6) were first generation Americans whose parents had emigrated from Greece in the early 20th Century. In 1915, Alex's mother had crossed the Atlantic on a vessel that stopped to pick up survivors of the RMS Lusitania, torpedoed and sunk in 18 minutes by a German U-boat. Alex's parents settled in Chicago, and it was there that they met (both parents would live to be 98). Proud to be newly-minted Americans, and wanting their children to fully assimilate into the American way of life, they never spoke Greek in their home.

Alex Athans in Vietnam. Photo provided.

The family eventually moved to Crystal Lake, Illinois, where Alex began high school, pitching on the baseball team as a freshman. Following his freshman year, the Athans went west, to Inglewood, California. After completing high school, Alex attended junior college from 1959-62 at El Camino Real and Los Angeles City College, concentrating on his general education requirements. In a youth group organization at his church, Alex met Patricia Peters, and they married in June 1963. The young married couple settled down in Glendale, and Alex went to work for a finance company in downtown Los Angeles. By the fall of 1965, Alex and Patricia (an elementary school teacher) had saved enough money to put a down payment on a home in La Crescenta.

By now, U.S. involvement in Vietnam was well underway and, in December 1965, Alex was drafted into the Army. Alex got good marks on his initial military testing and, as a result, was placed on an

An 8-inch howitzer in Vietnam.

officer track requiring a three-year service commitment (instead of the normal two-year commitment for draftees). Because of a spinal meningitis outbreak at Fort Ord, California, basic training was moved to Fort Bliss, Texas; in fact, Alex's company was the first to go through basic at Fort Bliss since the end of World War II. He recalled: "Basic training is always the same—very little sleep, lots of harassment! On the other hand, the harassment had a purpose; it was a way to get 250 men who came from all walks of life, from just about every state in the union, to work together."

Following basic training, Alex transferred to Fort Dix, New Jersey, for advanced infantry training (AIT) ("just like basic training with less harassment"). In the summer of 1966, he moved on to Fort Sill, Oklahoma, and was assigned to "B" Battery, 1st Battalion, 83rd Artillery, the battalion being reactivated for the first time since WWII. The battery boasted two 8-inch howitzers and two 175mm cannon; all the guns were self-propelled. All 135 men in "B" battery went through their artillery training at Fort Sill.

On October 13, 1966, the entire 83rd Artillery shipped out for Vietnam from the Oakland Army Terminal in two large transport ships. "When our ship [the USS Patrick Henry] went under the Golden Gate Bridge, a lot of the faces on the young men changed from boys to men, wondering if they'd ever see that bridge again." Before shipping out, Alex had been part of an advance party that went by train to the Oakland Army Terminal, along the way passing through Tehachapi.

On October 31st, Alex's transport reached Vietnam. For the following year, "B" battery went wherever it was needed to provide artillery

A 175mm cannon of Alex's 1st Battalion in action in Vietnam.

support for Army and Marine Corps units ("we were like a band of brothers"). Alex performed many different tasks in the battery, including loading the guns and also keeping a diary of battery activities (e.g., personnel changes, number of rounds fired on a given day, changes in location). For its sterling record of service, "B" Battery was mentioned on the Huntley-Brinkley Report as one of the outstanding heavy artillery batteries in the U.S. Army; in fact, the battery fired over 60,000 rounds in Alex's year of service.

In November 1967, Alex said goodbye to "B" Battery and Vietnam, flying into the major Air Force hub at Travis AFB, California, and then being bussed to San Francisco Airport. In uniform and waiting for his plane to take him home, he was harassed and "spit on a couple of times" by a group of anti-war protestors, who also ripped his uniform jacket. After a short 15-day leave, Alex was assigned to another heavy artillery unit (this time at Fort Bragg, North Carolina), which was earmarked for deployment to Vietnam. Fortuitously, however, Alex was transferred out of the artillery unit before it was dispatched overseas.

Alex was mustered out of the Army in February 1969, having attained the rank of Staff Sergeant (E-6). The Army had decided not to make him an officer because he failed to pass the physical for officers—his right leg was ½ inch shorter than his left! "God must have been with me because the life of a 2nd Lieutenant in Vietnam was not very long, especially in the infantry. So the Army did me a favor."

Back in La Crescenta, Alex initially had trouble finding work: "I was still not completely settled down from the experience in Vietnam. It was mostly my fault for memories I was carrying and not able to shake so soon after getting out of the service." He finally found employment with a bank, only to be fired when they discovered he was a Vietnam veteran. From 1969-80 he worked at several different jobs ("for anybody who would hire me"), mostly with finance companies or banks. Finally, he decided to "take control of my own life" by becoming self-employed as a general contractor, first in La Crescenta then in Tehachapi, having moved there in August 2000. Alex and Patricia soon fell in love with the town: "We love the open spaces and the four seasons. The people are polite and courteous. We couldn't have found a nicer place to live than Tehachapi." Alex retired in 2014, after working as a general contractor for more than 30 years.

On one occasion some years ago, Alex walked into a Sizzler's Restaurant in Bakersfield, where he stumbled upon a group of about 15 disabled Vietnam veterans. One of them had served with the 173rd Airborne in Vietnam and lost both of his legs during heavy combat in the summer of 1967. Talking with Alex, the man soon realized that it was Alex's battery that had saved his life at the time. During their impromptu discussion, Alex knelt in front of the disabled veteran's wheelchair. "He said, 'thanks for saving my ass.' I could feel the tears rolling down his face onto my hands, and now I know why I was there."

Alex and Pat, now married for 57 years, had two children, Christina and Gregory (when the children were young, Alex coached both soccer and Little League baseball). In 2012, Christina was diagnosed with pancreatic cancer, passing away two years later after a brave and gallant struggle. Several days before she died, she took her father aside: "Dad, let's face it, we're not in Disneyland here. I know I'm going to die. You know I'm going to die. I want you and mom to see that people donate money to pancreatic cancer research."

Alex and Pat not only honored their daughter's final request, they began highly successful annual fundraisers for pancreatic cancer research (sponsored by the Major Jason E. George VFW), in which 100% of the money raised was donated to the Pancreatic Cancer Action Network (all expenses are paid for by the Athans themselves). In the six years since Christina's passing, the fund raisers have generated about $118,000. In terms of individual donations to the PCAN, Christina ranks No. 1 in money raised; she also ranks No. 1 for raising the most money in the shortest amount of time. Indeed, the CEO of the PCAN is "just flabbergasted by what our little town has done."

Finally, it should be mentioned that, for the past three years, Alex has assisted the Veterans' Administration in counseling veterans in East Kern County.

Alex Athans—We honor you for your stalwart service to our country, and for all you've done to help those suffering from pancreatic cancer and veterans suffering from PTSD. You, Sir, are a True American Hero!

CHAPTER 14

Todd Lander: Combat Infantryman with the Elite 101st Airborne Division

(Note: Charles Loy "Todd" Lander passed away on August 24, 2021, after a year-long battle with cancer. For reasons that will remain unsaid, this author has removed his article on Todd from this book. Todd's story was one of the more significant stories in this volume, as it offered the reader a graphic, first-hand account of what infantry combat was like in Vietnam along the forward edge of battle. One can still read my original article in the July 31-August 14, 2021 issue of "The Loop Newspaper" (*Todd Lander—With the Elite 101st Airborne Division in Vietnam*). Simply "plug in" the title of the article on the web, or go directly to https://www.theloopnewspaper.com.)

That duly noted, this author would be guilty of an unforgivable oversight if he didn't inform you, dear reader, of the excellent Vietnam War memoir published by Todd Lander shortly before his passing. Todd's award-winning book, *Bound by War: A Memoir of Love, Friendship and Survival*, was released by virtualbookworm.com in July 2020. It is a beautifully written memoir that literally grabs the reader by the

Troops of the 101st Airborne Division in Vietnam. Todd Lander fought with the famous "Screaming Eagles" in "Nam" from July 1968 to July 1969

throat and drags him down into the steaming jungles and rice paddies of the killing fields of Vietnam in the late 1960s, when the tragic conflict that claimed the lives of 58,000 young American men was at its peak of violence, destruction, and death. Todd's book (available on Amazon.com) is one of the finest war memoirs this author has read in more than five decades of studying, researching, and writing about wars in the last two centuries; in fact, there were times when, after reading a particularly visceral and violent chapter, I had no choice but to put the book down—if only for a short while—to collect my own feelings and emotions.

To give readers further insight into Todd's magnificent book, this author has posted three reviews of *Bound by War*:

1. Martin Hernandez, Review of *Bound by War*, by Todd Lander, Amazon, August 21, 2020,

http://www.amazon.com/gp/customer-reviews/R4US9FU1KNKKV/ref=cm_cr_dp_d_rvw_ttl?ie=UTF8&ASIN=B08DLBVPWY.

"Gives such depth to personal memories—Excellent Book!
"BOUND BY WAR was a spectacular book on so many fronts. If you

lived through the trying times of the '60s, you will certainly remember the Vietnam War and how it affected you personally. Todd Lander's book about his personal experiences has captured a look into the past that too many had to endure, the bonds that were forged in that foreign land, the families and loved ones left behind, and a deep faith in God that carried them through.

Troops of 101st Airborne Division in a Landing Zone northwest of Dak To (June 1968)

"I remember all too well seeing my friends and classmates enlist, be drafted and go off to a war in a foreign land that they, themselves could not have fathomed. They left as mere teenagers and returned matured beyond their years, scarred for life, physically, emotionally and psychologically. Few talked about their experiences, harboring their emotions and not wanting to remember what had happened while abroad. Those changes left many of us at home bewildered with no understanding of what they went through.

"Todd Lander has bravely and brilliantly shared with the reader his personal story, his descriptive account of the tumultuous and horrific year in 'Nam. His writings wove into my memories a deeper understanding of the path endured by so many. This book moved my soul, my heart, and gave me such an immense feeling of gratitude for our Veterans. I will never see them as anything other than true

Heroes. Thank you for your service Todd, and for sharing your story and memorializing your friends in such an honorable way! Brilliantly written!"

2. "Zin" (the reviewer), Review of *Bound by War,* by Todd Lander, Amazon, August 22, 2021,

http://www.amazon.com/gp/customer-reviews/R2VR8C70F0XZ2Y/ref=cm_cr_dp_d_rvw_ttl?ie=UTF8&ASIN=B08DLBVPWY.

"Vietnam Page Turner: *Bound by War*

"I don't normally read books about war. This book, however, is about a war my friends and I lived through. I remember how the guys would come home and shrug off questions. We learned not to ask but could see that they were forever changed. Now, in vivid, very personally told detail, I understand their silence. I can feel the author's surroundings, friendships, fear, love, and faith. My heart breaks for his every loss and is relieved by every close call. This book is a page-turner that not only enlightens us to the raw details of the war but includes a love story with actual letters sent home to a new bride. We can also feel how the unspoken camaraderie of his company is far deeper in meaning than the war itself.

"Lander's writing is deceptively simple with smooth flowing dialog and explanations of the workings of military life in 1968. Descriptions of landscape and surroundings puts us right there in Vietnam, sleeping in the water of the rice paddies, removing leeches every morning, and coursing paths through jungles and across rivers. From story to story, told in short, succinct chapters, we learn about the ammunition, food, camps and sleeping arrangements. We learn what they packed, about the nighttime watches, how they moved, tactics, how they did or did not survive. Landers' year in Vietnam is chronicled with moments of humor and local human interest and his own love story but primarily it is one frightening drama after another, never winding down. This book is an eye-opener for those of us who did not go, and I am so grateful to have read it."

3. John Stanley, Review of *Bound by War*, by Todd Lander, Amazon, August 14, 2020,

http://www.amazon.com/gp/customer-reviews/R3NG00HC42V53M/ref=cm_cr_dp_d_rvw_ttl?ie=UTF8&ASIN=B08DLBVPWY

"A Remarkable Memoir of War and Love

"Visceral yet thought provoking. Amusing yet emotionally draining. Hopeful in the midst of hopelessness. Painful yet punctuated by moments of joy. Todd Lander has written one of the best war memoirs I have read. This easily belongs next to Tim O'Brien's, *The Things They Carried* as one of the best books of a line soldier's experience in Vietnam.

"Todd gives us short chapters that are vivid snapshots of his Vietnam experience. But they do not exist in isolation. He uses the letters his wife Sandy preserved that he sent her from his year there, as well as after-action reports from the battles in which he participated, to place both a broader context and a more intimate one on the things he experienced. He also masterfully integrates the episodes of his youth into his experiences in Vietnam.

"His prose is powerful and its imagery carries you into the rice patties, bomb craters and jungles of his experience in a way that captures all the fear and terror of his combat experience.

101st Airborne Division Patch (Vietnam Era)

“But it is the losses that will particularly stick with you. All the soldiers he remembered, who we get to know and who we experience losing for the first time as Todd recounts how he lost them. Their loss and his experiences exacted quite a price. The young man who landed in Vietnam as an FNG may have come home, but a part of him never returned from that country and it has taken him a lifetime to come to terms with the soldier who landed back in the world in San Francisco and had to run through a gauntlet of anti-war protesters jeering and spitting at him.

“This superbly written book will genuinely move you and will fill you with a deep respect for all those who served in this terrible war. I know several Vietnam vets and have been with them when they encounter one another who served there wearing a hat commemorating their time of service and sacrifice. They all greet each other with two words, 'Welcome home!' After reading Todd’s book, I have a far deeper appreciation of just what and how much this greeting means to these.

“*Bound by War* is indeed a book about love, friendship and survival.”

CHAPTER 15

Marsha Parker:
Story of a Gallant Army Nurse (1)

As always, we begin at the beginning: Marsha was born in 1946 in a little town in Ohio. Her father, a former Marine who had served in the Pacific theater in World War II, passed away at the age of 34 (like many Marines, he had contracted malaria during the war, and that had contributed to his tragic early death). Marsha was only 10 at the time and her mother, a stay-at-home mom, went to school after her husband's death to become a hairdresser. "That is how she supported us until she remarried," Marsha said. Marsha attended high school in Upper Sandusky, also a small town in Ohio, graduating in 1964. While in high school, she worked at the

Marsha Parker getting her bars and being sworn in. Photo provided.

local hospital—in the lab, the laundry, in housekeeping, "wherever there was a little job for a high school kid."

Interested in becoming a nurse from an early age, she took part in a three-year nursing program in Lima, Ohio, graduating in 1967 with a general degree in nursing. She then went back to work at the little hospital in Upper Sandusky, but only for a few weeks. "All of us in nursing school," Marsha said, "were well aware of what was going on in Vietnam. We knew there was a shortage of nurses. Several guys from my town had been killed in Vietnam. And, remember, at that time, patriotism meant serving. So I felt called to serve in the military."

Marsha joined the Army in late 1967 ("it was Army all the way!"). Basic training took place at Fort Sam Houston, San Antonio, Texas. "I don't know if people realize that even nurses [in basic] are put through field exercises. We had to run a map course, to learn how to find our way around with a compass if we were lost in the middle of nowhere. It was a bunch of young women, not all in the greatest shape, trying to find their way back to base; about two-thirds made it back, the others had to be rescued! During basic, our platoon leader was an older, experienced surgical nurse. She kind of held us all together. She would lead us on marches around the quad and shout out orders, including one she had made up: 'hippity hop platoon stop!' This drove our drill sergeants nuts, and she'd do it to antagonize them. When one of them [protested] she would respond: 'my dear, you need to watch your blood pressure!' Eventually, they threw up their hands and let her do what she wanted. We had discipline, but not quite the kind of discipline the drill sergeants wanted us to have."

During basic training, to prepare the nurses for what was to come, they had to practice on goats shot with high-velocity weapons (such as an AK-47), learning how to stop bleeding, suture and close up wounds, remove dead tissue, etc. "When you shoot something with a high-velocity weapon, it literally explodes the tissue, blood vessels, nerves inside the body. That's why they did it. They wanted to show us how to deal with those kinds of wounds. All of us came out of that a little shocked. Most of us had never seen anything like that." After basic training, Marsha was assigned to Fort Belvoir, Virginia, working in

Marsha Parker in Vietnam. Photo provided.

orthopedics. Two months later, she got her orders for Vietnam.

Marsha went to Vietnam in early 1968, at the time of the massive Tet Offensive launched by Viet Cong guerillas and North Vietnamese regulars and resulting in a sharp decline in support for the war among the American people. She was assigned to the 71st Evacuation Hospital in Pleiku, which also hosted an Army division and an Air Force base. The hospital included medevac helicopter pads, an emergency receiving area, surgical and recovery units, and rows of medical surgical facilities each with 40 patients. As Marsha recalled, "The medics on board the medevac helos—we called them 'dust off' units—were amazing; by the time the wounded reached us, 75% of them had been stabilized." And because the medical care provided by Marsha, the other nurses, and doctors was so good, 92% of the wounded would survive their injuries.

Following a thorough orientation to familiarize the mostly inexperienced nurses with every facet of their job, Marsha was assigned to a med/surg (medical-surgical) unit. Because the wounds sustained by soldiers were dirty with debris and often contaminated with human or animal feces (e.g., from enemy booby traps), which could result in life-threatening infections, the surgical units employed a technique—delayed primary closure—that was experimental at the time, if now commonplace. "We would open the wound and put in a fine gauze. After it had dried and attached itself to the tissue, we'd tear it out, removing any debris or dead cells that were left. That was extremely successful for healthy healing. We saved a lot of arms and legs that way."

Marsha and her fellow nurses worked six 12-hour shifts a week, "unless there was a push, meaning we got unexpected volumes of wounded, then we'd work for 24 to 36 hours, or until we got everyone taken care of." Indeed, the duties of a nurse in Vietnam were relentless, unforgiving, and, at Pleiku, often interrupted by enemy mortar attacks, which resulted in no loss of life during Marsha's time there. "A lot of the nurses," she recalled, "came back from Vietnam with PTSD. And I see that same look on the faces of the nurses now working with Covid-19."

At Pleiku, Marsha met the singer and actress, Martha Raye, who came through the hospital on several occasions "and really brightened up the troops. She was a very unique woman. She was intensely involved with the troops in the field and made many trips to Vietnam. She was out to save each and every guy." (Note: Ms. Raye became a colonel in the Army Reserve, and is the only woman buried in the special forces cemetery at Fort Bragg, North Carolina.) While in Vietnam, Marsha also met her first husband, an Army helicopter pilot.

After being out processed from the military, Marsha returned to the States in early 1969. She went to work as a civilian nurse at Fort Sill, Oklahoma, and, in the years that followed, accompanied her Army husband to other bases, working in doctors' offices and hospitals. While at Edwards Air Force Base in the late 1970s, Marsha went back to school, eventually earning a BA in archaeology from the

University of Maryland and an MA in health services administration from Chapman University in southern California (1984). Along the way, she had two children: Chris, a boy, born in 1969; and Kelly, a girl, born in 1974. (Following a divorce, Marsha remarried in 1990.)

Also in the late 1970s, Marsha began her participation in a decades-long military study driven in part by concerns about exposure to the defoliant Agent Orange and the long-term impact of PTSD (the study was recently published). Near the end of the study, one of her interviewers observed, "You are the one person I've interviewed who has seemed to become stronger over the years." Marsha attributed this to the wonderful support she had received from back home: Marsha had been taken by the plight of the local Montagnard villagers and had done all she could to help them (as had many other nurses). "I was lucky enough to link up with the special forces in Pleiku, and when they went out, I just went with them [into the villages]." When the folks in Upper Sandusky got wind of Marsha's charity, they responded by sending all kinds of supplies—soaps, bandages, bedding, iodine, anything they thought might be of help to the Montagnards. "I was in

Marsha Parker and her husband. Photo provided.

despair sometimes looking at how horrible the lives of some of these people were, then looking at our own guys, and how bad off they were. But I never fell into the depression and hopelessness that some of my colleagues did. Some of the nurses were overwhelmed because they felt they could never do enough for the men. They never had the kind of support system I had."

While her first husband was stationed at Edwards AFB, Marsha had worked at Antelope Valley Hospital. During that time, she had gotten to know some people from Tehachapi and learned a little about the town. After remarrying, she and her husband moved to Bear Valley Springs in 2002.

Marsha—you are a true American patriot, and we salute you for your brave and selfless service to our country!

CHAPTER 16

Doug McHenry: Air Force B-52 Bomber Crew Chief

Doug McHenry was born in Chicago, Illinois, on October 5, 1947, right about 12:00 noon. His mother liked to tease him that she missed Sunday dinner because of his birth! Doug was an only child. While the family lived in Gary, Indiana (until 1960), Doug's father worked in construction in Chicago, helping to build tall commercial buildings and churches. As Doug recollected, "my father would put the lath up on the walls or columns, and create window openings for churches. He loved his work. He was an artist of sorts." In fact, building and constructing things went back for generations in Doug's family: "Most of us were tradesmen or craftsmen."

Yet by early 1960, construction work had temporarily dried up in the "Windy City," so in April of that year, the family headed for San Diego, California, so Mr. McHenry could find construction work. Doug's dad came out to San Diego first to look for housing and secure a job; his wife and son followed on the train from Chicago.

Doug, now a young teenager, had developed a passion for cars and hot rods, so he was thrilled to move to California, "the capital of hot rodding." "When the train pulled in to San Bernadino, I thought I had died and gone to heaven. Parked across the street from the train switchyard was a 1951 or 1952 customized Chevy! But in the 8th Grade, my English teacher told me and a friend we'd never amount to anything because of our love of cars and hot rods!" Little did she know!

Mr. McHenry found another lathing job in San Diego, while Doug attended Clairemont High School in the city, graduating in 1965. Doug wasn't interested in making a big "splash" in high school; he wasn't a "jock" or all that social. As he put it: "I was still neck deep in hot rods!" After graduation, Doug went to work at a gas station, then as a receiving inspector for Control Data Corporation. After work, he'd meet other car enthusiasts at Oscar's Drive-In, and from there, they'd go out to drag race. Yet slowly, he began to notice that there were fewer and fewer folks his age at the drive-in—they'd either enrolled in college or joined a branch of the service, for American military involvement in Vietnam was escalating.

Having no plan to go on to college, Doug decided to join the Air Force, enlisting in December 1966. On his military aptitude testing, he scored "off the charts" (95th percentile) for mechanical skills, opening up all kinds of career fields to him. "I could basically choose any career field I wanted. I chose to be a machinist, because that would help me attain the skills I needed to open an auto speed shop after I got out of the service."

For Air Force recruits, basic training took place at Lackland AFB, Texas (and to this day, still does); yet after arriving there, Doug was disappointed to discover that the machinist career field was temporarily closed. As an alternative career field, he selected Aircraft Mechanic for jets with more than two engines, which essentially meant working with bomber and large transport aircraft.

After basic training, Doug was off to technical school at Chanute AFB, Illinois, which he completed in May 1967. Airman Second Class McHenry was then assigned to March AFB in Riverside, California. By 1969, he had become a crew chief for a B-52 "Stratofortress" strategic bomber of the 22nd Bomb Wing, whose mission included nuclear alert (this was just a few years after the Cuban Missile Crisis and the Cold War with the Soviet Union was still quite "hot.") As Doug recalled, "I loved the B-52. To this day I love the airplane. It was a fantastic airplane. If I could drop my crutches, I'd still fly on one. It was an incredibly reliable airplane." In the meantime, Doug had also fallen in love with a young lady, tying the knot in March 1967.

B-52 bombers drop 1000lb bombs during Operation Arc Light.

The marriage—although eventually ending in divorce—brought forth three sons, in 1968, 1969, and 1971.

While stationed at March AFB, Doug went TDY to Guam, Okinawa, and Thailand, in support of B-52 "Arc Light" operations in Vietnam. (During Arc Light from 1965 to 1973, US Air Force B-52 bombers, operating out of Guam, conducted air strikes on enemy bases, supply lines, and troop concentrations, on occasion even providing close air support for Army and Marine Corps ground troops.) His first TDY to Guam took place in early 1968. "North Vietnamese regulars had attacked the Marine base at Khe Sanh. Our bombers and tankers flew round the clock, seven days a week, for two weeks solid. We were so busy doing maintenance, or launching and recovering aircraft that we hardly ever got off the ramp. We got sleep when we could. It was a baptism by fire. You really found out who pulled his weight and who didn't. It was the only place I learned to sleep standing up in a B-52 wheel well for protection during a monsoon."

Doug had many memorable experiences while serving at March AFB, but there was one in particular that still stands out: "In the summer of '68, I went home for the weekend to see my parents in San Diego. I walked in the door and one of my best friends from high school was there. I said, 'hey, how are you doing?' He replied, 'I just got back from Vietnam. I'm in the Marines.' I didn't know this as I hadn't seen him since we graduated high school. He asked me what I was doing. I said, 'I just got home from Guam, I was supporting Arc Light operations.' At that, his eyes got big; he said, 'I was at Khe Sanh. You saved my life.' It almost brought me to tears."

Doug departed March AFB in May 1970 and was reassigned to Chanute AFB as an instructor for aircraft maintenance (for jets over two engines). "My time at Chanute as an instructor helped to change my life. It taught me how to cross my 'Ts' and dot my 'Is.' I learned to never open my mouth unless I could back it up—that has been a Godsend to me for the rest of my life. As an instructor, you take a person from the unknown to the known, and it's an incredible feeling to watch the transformation of that individual as he learns his craft."

In December 1972, Staff Sergeant McHenry was assigned to Travis AFB, California, to this day a major Air Force transportation hub. Once again, he had the major responsibility of a crew chief—this time for a massive C-5 "Galaxy" transport. Unlike the B-52, however, Doug despised the C-5! As he explained it, the aircraft was mechanically unreliable and, thus, frustrating to work on; moreover, he found the culture in Military Airlift Command to be much more casual ("there was much less discipline") than in Strategic Air Command. "It was just mass insanity. Nothing made sense to me at all! On one occasion, a C-5 crew held up their flight to Vietnam because they hadn't received their hot coffee, when they could have made it themselves in their own galley!"

Less than a year later (September 1973), Doug was mustered out of the Air Force. Although on track to become a technical sergeant, he turned down the potential promotion. "If I had re-enlisted, I would have made technical sergeant within a year, but I also would have been locked in for about five years working on C-5s at Travis, and I didn't want to do that. This was a pivotal time. If I hadn't gotten out then, it would most likely have been in for 20 years."

The U.S. Air Force's C-17 "Globemaster" transport aircraft.

After leaving the Air Force, Doug was able to parlay his military experience into a highly active and remunerative professional life. At first, he went back to San Diego, working for several Ford dealerships and becoming a jack of all trades—"I became a bumper to bumper mechanic, I did it all!" After leaving Ford in the mid-1980s ("I got tired of the automobile repair business, got kind of burned out"), he took a position with Rockwell International, working in Lancaster on the B-1 Bomber program.

In 1988, Doug remarried, he and his second wife having two more children ("we had seven children in our blended family, as my wife came to the marriage with two of her own"). The next year (1989), he joined Douglas Aircraft, working on the C-17 transport and other aircraft as a flight test mechanic. Laid off from Douglas in 1994, he went to work for the famous Lockheed-Martin "Skunk Works" in Palmdale for several years. "I can't tell you what I did at Lockheed. If I did, I'd have to kill ya! It was really secret stuff."

Several years later (1997), the peripatetic Mr. McHenry moved on to yet another position, this time employed by the California Department of Corrections at their correctional facility in El Centro as an automotive instructor. He worked there for two years. In 1999, Doug received an offer to transfer to the correctional facility just outside Tehachapi. He jumped at the opportunity. "Tehachapi was a pretty area, close to Lancaster where we lived, and it wasn't El Centro!" In 2004, having caught the "Tehachapi bug," Doug purchased a home in nearby Stallion Springs.

Medically retired since 2012 due to work-related injuries, Doug continues to enjoy his retirement playing with his hot rods and race cars!

Doug McHenry—We honor you for your selfless service to our great nation in times of war and peace!

CHAPTER 17

Diane Tharp:
Story of a Gallant Army Nurse (2)

Diane was born in Lancaster, Pennsylvania, on December 12, 1943. When she was very young, she moved with her parents to Wilmington, Delaware. Her father, an electrician, made a career with Delaware Power & Light, while her mother was a stay-at-home mom. When Diane was just 10 years old, tragedy struck, her father dying suddenly. "It was a tough time," she recalled, "and mom had to go to work. She worked in a pharmacy."

Diane Tharp in Vietnam. Photo provided.

After her mother remarried, the family moved to Newark, Delaware. Diane attended John Dickinson High School in Wilmington (just a "hop, skip, and a jump" from Newark), and was drawn to the fields of science and nursing. "I wanted to become a nurse. I always wanted to help people. When I was a little girl, I put bandaids on everything!"

After graduating from high school in 1961, Diane matriculated at Delaware Hospital School of Nursing (also in Wilmington). "It wasn't like nursing school today. We had house mothers. We had to be in our rooms by 10:00 p.m., with lights out by 10:30 p.m. It was very strict. If we wanted to study past 10:30, we'd hide in our closets and shove a towel in the bottom of the door so the light didn't show." She completed her nursing studies in 1964 and was employed by Delaware Hospital as a nurse for several years.

In 1965, Diane made the decision to join the National Guard in Delaware. "I was doing it for the money," she said, "that's an honest answer." In an unusual move, the Guard detailed her to Fort Sam Houston in San Antonio, Texas, for six weeks of basic training; to this day, she has no idea why the Guard sent her to basic (typical Guard service was simply two weekends a month, then an extended two-week period of service at some point in a given year).

Yet the opportunity to go through basic training was very much to Diane's benefit. "There was so much to learn. How the military did things. During basic, they'd shoot the goats that were out in the fields, then we'd learn how to remove the bullets and stitch them up." When she returned from San Antonio, she was able to teach the two other nurses in her Guard unit what she had learned.

Meanwhile, the Vietnam War was heating up, and Diane's experiences at basic training had aroused her interest in adventure and traveling. So, Diane joined the Army. As noted, she had always wanted to help people; now, she wanted to go to Vietnam to do just that. As she said, "I thought I could really help there."

A young woman in her early 20s, Diane flew from Travis AFB to Vietnam in August 1967. The great adventure had indeed begun, even if, at first, it made her question her sanity! "When I got off the transport in Saigon, they put us on buses that looked like prison busses. We were escorted by jeeps mounted with .50 caliber heavy machine guns." Struggling to grasp the reality of it all, she asked herself: "What is a nice girl like me doing in a place like this! To this day, I remember saying that to myself!"

Diane was assigned to the 2nd Surgical Hospital in Chulai. Like most nurses in Vietnam, she worked 12 hours shifts and, when overwhelmed by large numbers of wounded coming in from the field, she and other nurses worked around the clock until the crisis was overcome. Diane worked mostly at night, "that's when we got patients who had been stabilized ready for transport to Ramstein, Germany, for long-term care. Over 90 percent of our patients [at Chulai] survived their wounds. However, at Chulai we had no assigned neurosurgeon, so we had to wait for the arrival of the Navy hospital ship that would provide us with a neurosurgeon. As a result, most of the wounded who required a neurosurgeon didn't make it."

Among her many experiences in Chulai, two came quickly to mind. "We had a patient come in who had been shot in the buttocks. He was a sergeant. He had a wife and two kids at home. He was bleeding profusely. We couldn't stop the bleeding. He looked up at me and said, 'Am I going to be OK?' I said, 'You're going to be just fine.' Two minutes later, he was gone. That disturbed me, whether I'd done the right thing. Another patient, who I adored, had also been shot in the buttocks; he survived and I helped him, when he was unable to do so himself, by writing letters for him to his girlfriend back home."

After some four months in Chulai, Diane was transferred to a military hospital in An Khe, where she worked from late 1967 to the spring of 1968. She then moved on to a new military hospital in Da Nang, where—to put it gently—she made quite an impression one day on General William Westmoreland, Commander of U.S. forces in Vietnam from 1964-1968. General Westmoreland was in Da Nang, visiting troops, wounded soldiers, and nurses there. As Diane explained, when

Diane Tharp outside one of the hospital units. Notice the sandbags and large drums in place to defend against attack. Photo provided.

the "brass" came through, "making the rounds," passing out Purple Hearts, medals, etc., all personnel were simply to continue with their normal duties. Diane was standing on a crate, reaching for an item on a shelf. She suddenly turned around and saw the general standing two feet away from her. Looking up at her on the crate, he quipped, "You certainly are a tall nurse!" Without a moment's hesitation, Diane shot back, "You certainly are a small general!"

Diane, of course, was shocked by her "impudence," though her response wasn't meant to be mean-spirited in any way. "If only I could have taken back those words. I was so embarrassed. I wanted to crawl through the floorboards!" Yet, no worries, for the good general took no offense and simply laughed it off, much to Diane's relief. "No one at the time, however, thought it was funny, except for the general. I think if he hadn't laughed it off, I'd still be in Fort Leonard Wood with a ball and chain around my ankle!"

In late August 1968, Diane returned to the States and was again assigned to Fort Sam Houston in Texas. In August 1969, she was mustered out of the Army and moved to Madera, California, working for less than a year at Dearborn General Hospital there. This was followed by a move to a hospital in Las Vegas, Nevada, where she was assigned to an operating room. After five or six years in Las Vegas, she decided to return to California. In 1980, she married her husband, Lee, and they would have three children together. In 2014, Diane retired from the nursing profession.

A few years earlier (about 2010), Diane received a telephone call "out of the blue" from the television series, Mail Call, hosted by R. Lee Ermey, a retired U.S. Marine Corps staff sergeant and honorary gunnery sergeant. During each episode (the show debuted in 2002), Ermey read and responded to questions submitted by viewers about weapons, military equipment, customs, and terminology used by the U.S. military. More to the point, Diane was asked to come on the show and speak about the experiences of nurses in Vietnam, which she readily did. Yet to this day she has no idea how they got hold of her.

Reflecting on her year of service in Vietnam, Diane said, "Basically there were such highs and such lows, but it was the best nursing I ever did. We saved a lot of lives. It was the best, and the worst, year of my life." While in Vietnam, and in the decades of civilian life that followed, Diane, unlike many Vietnam nurses, was not affected by PTSD. "I have a really good sense of humor," she said. "So I was more resilient. It wasn't until some five or six years ago, after bottling it all up inside for so long, that I began to have some of my own issues." Fortunately for Diane, she sought help from the Veterans Administration. "I got some counseling. And that was very helpful."

To conclude my interview with this delightful lady, I should note that Diane remains a proud, patriotic American, who is not shy about defending her country, our troops, and, most importantly, the memories of the wounded (and dying) young men to whom she was so fully committed as a veritable "Angel of Mercy." Diane brought this home "in spades" with this anecdote: "I was in a quilting group a few years back with several other women, about 10. One of the ladies, who had never served in Vietnam, but thought she knew everything about that war—well, she just went on and on, often disrespecting our troops with her comments. Eventually, I couldn't tolerate her ignorance any longer. So, I stood up and I said, 'You've never been to Vietnam and you're just full of shit.' She shut up. I loved the boys I helped over there."

And, Diane Tharp, we love you as well—for your selfless and gallant service to a nation that will never forget you.

CHAPTER 18

Barry Bongberg: Avionics Repairman & Helicopter Door Gunner

"As we landed in Cam Ranh Bay, Vietnam, our commanding officer gave us a little welcoming address. 'Now boys, I want you to shake the hands of the person on your left and right. One won't be going home alive, the other will return wounded, or diseased. Good luck.' This little speech hit us all with the true realities of fear and confusion. This just could not be happening. It was all happening much too fast." (*Dear Mom & Dad. Letters Home from Vietnam, 1967-1969*, by Barry Bongberg, ix)

Barry Bongberg sitting on a helicopter seat and taking a break from his repair work at his base near Chu Lai. Photo provided.

Barry was born on October 30, 1948. At the time, his father, a World War II veteran—as were both his brothers and sister, a nurse at Pearl Harbor on December 7, 1941—was enrolled in dental school at the University of Pennsylvania. Barry's mother was a stay-at-home mom (her brother had also served in WWII). Barry had two siblings—an older brother and a younger sister, who died of breast cancer in 2009.

In the early 1950s, the Bongberg family moved to Oregon, where Dr. Bongberg was employed by the state as a dentist. A short time later (1954), they moved on to Shafter, where Barry grew up from the 2nd Grade through high school. At Shafter High School, he played junior varsity football for three years. He spent the summer between his junior and senior years picking lemons in Santa Barbara. As Barry recalled that summer with a twinkle in his eye, "it was in Santa Barbara that I discovered girls and beer!"

"I had a great childhood in Shafter," he said. "I was in the Boy Scouts. Dad took us hunting and fishing. It was a wonderful place to grow up. I had a righteous family. A strong work ethic was instilled in us kids; if I wanted new clothes, I had to buy them myself."

Barry was just 17 when he graduated from high school in 1966. In the fall of that year, he enrolled at Bakersfield Community College; yet as he openly admitted, he wasn't a serious student, and after a short time, he stopped attending most of his classes. His brother, a Marine, was already in Vietnam, as were his two best friends (also Marines). "At least I had the sense to know I wasn't going anywhere with my life. I had no ambition for school. So in December 1966, I went down to the Federal Building on Truxton Avenue in Bakersfield and volunteered for the draft."

In February 1967, shortly after his 18th birthday, he was inducted into the Army. At Fort Lewis, Washington, he got high marks on his testing and, as a result, was given the chance to go to signal school at Fort Gordon, Georgia—keeping him out of the infantry—in exchange for agreeing to an extra (3rd) year of active duty in the Army. Barry readily accepted the Army's offer, but first up was basic training, which took place at Fort Leonard Wood, Missouri. At Fort Gordon, Barry trained to be a helicopter avionics equipment repairman (one of the training specialties offered at the signal school), completing the course in about five months.

The night before he left for Vietnam, Barry, a skinny, fun-loving teenager, painted the town with a good friend, getting "wasted" on beer. On October 25, 1967, he landed at Cam Ranh Bay, Vietnam, a massive military complex in an inlet of the South China Sea, with an air base, a naval yard, Army and Marine detachments.

Private First Class Bongberg was first assigned to the 123rd Aviation Company (449th Signal Detachment, 1st Aviation Brigade), a helicopter outfit south of Chu Lai in the I Corps sector, the northernmost corps sector in South Vietnam. Some months later, his company would be combined with the 723rd Maintenance Battalion, Americal Division, "but we didn't change our location. We just got a new mailing address."

Barry was soon doing maintenance on helicopter avionics and flying occasional missions as a door gunner. "As the months passed, some died, some were wounded and those surviving all tried to adapt in some crazy sort of way. This adapting was so scary. This miserable

The ammunition dump at Chu Lai—destroyed during the 1968 Tet Offensive. Photo Provided.

war was taking away our youthful aspirations and dreams. These long-forgotten desires had been replaced by the war realities of mud, blood, beer, rats, drugs and losses. We prayed, we laughed, we cried, we got high. Survival. We adapted." (*Dear Mom & Dad*, x)

The worst period of Barry's service in the Vietnam War came in late January and February 1968, when the Viet Cong and the North Vietnamese People's Army launched their spectacular Tet Offensive, striking targets across South Vietnam—a significant escalation of the war that had a major psychological impact on the American people and convinced President Lyndon B. Johnson not to run for reelection. At the onset of the enemy offensive, Barry and his fellow soldiers sheltered in their bunkers for several days. "They blew up the ammo dump at Chu Lai. We were being heavily shelled. Guys were screaming for their mothers. It was ugly. A Chinese rocket got stuck in a sandbag in the bunker behind us. It was a dud. If it had exploded, it would have taken us all out."

During his service in Vietnam, Barry stood guard duty on a regular basis, at times taking serious in-coming enemy fire. Moreover, he flew at least 10 missions as a helicopter door gunner, among them some extremely dangerous night missions. "It got to a point," he said, "where I had my superiors take me off the roster to fly as a door gunner. It was not in my MOS [Military Occupational Specialty], and it just got too dangerous."

After Barry had completed his year of service in Vietnam, he received orders to return to the States (Fort Benning, Georgia). However, despite the myriad dangers associated with service in a combat zone, Barry decided instead to extend his tour in Vietnam, which enabled him to qualify for an early discharge from the military. As he recalled, "by now, I was pretty acclimated to Vietnam, I was getting flight pay, combat pay, and I'd already advanced in rank to sergeant. I didn't want to do stateside duty, so I extended for six months."

In the spring of 1969, Barry extended his Vietnam service for an

The military base just outside Chu Lai where Barry Bongberg spent most of his 23 months of service in Vietnam. Photo provided.

additional five months—a decision which, due to recent changes in Army personnel policy, further reduced his active duty service commitment. On September 20, 1969, he penned his final letter to his parents: "I am now returning home after 23 months in this war. I am 20 years old with the rank of sergeant, having received three medals of commendation in the war. I'm still too young to vote and to buy beer back home. I will beat this last letter home." (Dear Mom & Dad, 132) (Note: His citations were: Meritorious Defense Service Medal; Vietnam Service Medal with two Oak Leaf Clusters; Vietnam Campaign Medal; Army Commendation Medal for Valor Against a Hostile Force.)

Returning to Fort Lewis, he was discharged from the Army. Well aware of the problems Vietnam veterans were now facing at home, he had the presence of mind to have his parents send him civilian clothes, so he wouldn't have to travel home in his uniform. "It was that ugly out there for us Vietnam vets."

Now more mature, more motivated, Barry got on with his life in a big way. He graduated from Santa Barbara Community College in 1972 with an Associate of Science (AS) degree in Business Administration. He then transferred to Fresno State University, picking up a BA in humanities and photography (1974).

From 1974 to 1983, he resided in Sonoma County (Santa Rosa, California), working initially as a professional photographer and later as a piano repairman. In 1978, he married Karen, and they soon had a daughter, Erica. When the marriage ended in divorce, Barry decided to return to Shafter.

In 1990, he completed his MA in Behavioral Science at California State University, Bakersfield. In the years that followed, Barry made a successful career in the field of health and human services, which included working as a counselor at several local prisons and, from 1994-2001, living in Alaska above the arctic circle and working with the mentally ill, drug addicts, and homeless. He retired in 2007 as a Supervising Mental Health Clinician in Kern County.

Which brings us back to Barry's book, *Dear Mom & Dad. Letters Home from Vietnam, 1967-1969.*

For more than 50 years, Barry had in his possession a box of letters he'd written to his mother and father from Vietnam. He'd begun writing to them within 24 hours of his arrival in-country and continued to compose letters to his parents—268 letters to be exact—throughout his almost two years in Southeast Asia.

But the letters had languished in their box—until recently, with the encouragement of his daughter, Erica, and the awareness of his advancing age, Barry decided it was time to open the box and begin to type the letters into a manuscript for Erica, her three children, and other loved ones. He typed them, word for word and, in early 2021, with the help of Ms. Sara Olsher (layout and design), published all of them in his book.

Only months before, Erica had lost her brave battle with breast cancer, passing away on September 17, 2020. In June 2019, Barry and his daughter had visited our nation's capital, guests of Honor Flight Kern County. "It was such a healing and precious experience to share together. It was the best father and daughter experience ever!"

(Note: Barry's wonderful book is available at Amazon.com. All proceeds are dedicated to the ongoing fight against breast cancer.)

CHAPTER 19

Michael Gillum:
From Combat Engineer to Mission of Reconciliation

Michael Gillum was born in Indianapolis, Indiana, on March 1, 1946. He belonged to a family of giants: his father was 6' 3" and his younger brother 6' 8" in height, while Michael himself grew to be 6' 6" tall (his older brother only made it to 6' 2"). His father served in the Army Air Forces (AAF) as an aircraft mechanic in WWII in the Italian theater of war, while Michael's mother was a stay-at-home mom. Following the war, his father worked various odd jobs, finally landing a position as a civilian mechanic at Kirtland Air Force Base, outside Albuquerque, New Mexico.

Michael Gillum at Basic Training at Fort Leonard Wood, Missouri. Photo provided.

When Michael was just five years old, his father rejoined the military (U.S. Air Force) and, in 1952, was assigned to Ramstein Air Base, West Germany (the ocean liner the family took to Germany followed in the wake of the RMS Queen Mary). Michael attended 1st through 4th grades in Germany.

After four years at Ramstein AB, in the late 1950s, the family moved on to Carswell Air Force Base, Texas. It was in Texas that Michael first experienced segregation and Jim Crow. "I saw white kids being taken off in their busses to white schools, and black kids to the black schools, all off the base. But on the base, we were all the same. We were neighbors. It seemed kind of crazy to me. All through my early years, my best friends were mostly Black, Hispanic, or Asian."

After several years at Carswell AFB, Michael's father was transferred to Edwards AFB, home of the Air Force Flight Test Center. Michael attended Desert High at Edwards from 1960 to 1964 and had a very active school life. He played basketball, volleyball, ran track, and was a member of the Latin and math clubs. He also played clarinet and tenor saxophone in the school band, touring much of Kern County and performing at halftimes of high school football games. The band also played at the annual summer parades in Boron, where, on one occasion, Ronald Reagan was the parade's grand marshal.

Michael matriculated at Valparaiso University, Indiana, receiving his BS in Civil Engineering in 1968. As he recalled, "Valparaiso was a Christian university, and my faith in Christ grew so strong that I had total trust in God to look out for me."

With his college degree in hand, Michael took a job in Los Angeles with the State of California, Division of Highways, as a highway engineer. However, he now faced a dilemma: He no longer enjoyed the student deferment he had in college, making him eligible for the draft at the height of the Vietnam War. What should he do? Instead of waiting to be drafted, Michael enlisted in the Army in July 1968, with the understanding that, by doing so, he would have more control over his experience in the service. His decision paid off, for the Army offered him a six-month deferment to continue working for the State of California.

In January 1969, Michael was formally inducted into the Army. Both his basic training and advanced infantry training (AIT) took place at Fort Leonard Wood, Missouri (or, as the recruits called it, "fort lost in the woods, misery!"). After AIT, he completed a non-commissioned officer (NCO) training course for combat engineers that had only recently been established at the base. "I attended the second class [of this new training course]. About 90 percent of those in the class were college graduates. We had a lot of 'brainiacs' in that class."

Michael was able to spend Christmas 1969 with his family. Then, in January 1970, the newly minted E-5 (Sergeant) was finally off to Vietnam. He was assigned to the 18th Engineering Brigade in Pleiku,

U.S. air base at Pleiku.

site of vital U.S. bases in the central highlands of Vietnam not far from the Cambodian border. As a construction foreman, Sergeant Gillum oversaw the construction of a major section of National Highway 14, a strategic highway that traversed central South Vietnam, connecting key towns and cities along the way (including Pleiku). Simply put, his mission was to transform a dirt road into a paved highway along a stretch of some 50 miles, while clearing out foliage and trees on either side of the new highway and building bridges across intersecting streams and rivers. "It was quite frightening, because there were woods on both sides of the road, and we could be ambushed at any time." Michael and his fellow combat engineers also built fire bases close to the Cambodian frontier and cleared mines off of dirt roads for vehicle convoys.

Michael would often inspect the work being done on the highway from the vantage point of a helicopter, which also gave him the opportunity to see firsthand the degradation of the environment caused by the war. "It was very disheartening to see the results of using the [chemical defoliant] Agent Orange. And also to see the bomb craters. It was unbelievable. They were everywhere. It was quite disturbing."

Interestingly, he noted that the inhabitants of the central and northern highlands of South Vietnam included more than 50 ethnic tribes, with customs and languages that differed from the Vietnamese people in general. As Michael explained, these tribes were quite primitive and were often treated as second-class citizens. "The Viet Cong would come into their villages and say, 'you will fight for us, or we will kill your families.' Then South Vietnamese soldiers would go into their villages and do the same. In some cases, these poor people would fight during the day for the South, and at night for the Viet Cong."

Michael experienced many traumatic events during his time in South Vietnam, but none more so than what took place on May 12, 1970. "Major-General [John A.B.] Dillard was in charge of all the engineering work in Vietnam. He came for a visit to inspect our projects. He was accompanied by high-ranking officers and NCOs from the brigade group and battalion HQ. Also with the general were the helicopter pilot, co-pilot, and two 19-year-old door gunners. I had lunch with the door gunners before the inspection. However, I was unable to go out with them due to the lack of room in the [UH-1 Huey] helicopter. So I stayed behind and monitored their radio communications. About 30 minutes after the two helos had left, a 'Mayday' distress call came in from the combat escort helo. He said that the Huey with the general and the two young door gunners had been shot down; 10 out of 11 men died. One of the door gunners [upon completion of his year of service in Vietnam] had been scheduled to return to the U.S. the next day."

Michael returned to the States after his tour of duty in early December 1970, flying into Travis AFB. When he exited the transport aircraft, the sergeant in charge quipped, "if you have any problems just learn to deal with them." Sergeant Gillum was officially mustered out of the Army on December 12, 1970.

He went back to work for the State of California. In 1971, he got married. He had met Carolyn, his future bride, at a Christmas party before going off to Vietnam, and during his time there, they had stayed in touch. Their marriage would bring forth three children—a boy (who grew to be 6'11" tall! and made a career in the Army) and two (much shorter) girls. (In 1995, following a divorce, Michael married Ginny.)

Laid off by the State of California in the mid-1970s, Michael found a position with the city of Richland's water and sewer department in eastern Washington State. He worked there for 25 years, retiring in 2001. The following year, after the death of his father, Michael and Ginny moved to the Antelope Valley to help care for his widowed mother.

Despite a successful career and his success as a devoted family man, Michael struggled—for years that soon stretched into decades—to come to terms with his service in Vietnam. "Since returning from Vietnam, there were aspects of my life I didn't fully understand.

There were times when I thought about suicide," he said. He went 42 years without seeking help, without saying anything to his parents, his siblings, to anyone. No doubt, like so many other Vietnam veterans battling PTSD, he simply "buried [himself] in his job."

Finally, in 2013, he began seeing a psychiatrist at the VA hospital in Sepulveda; telling his story, "getting it out," instead of futilely seeking to avoid the pain and anger, made a palpable difference for Michael, and he began his road to recovery. Late in 2013, he took another major step along that road—making the first of his five visits to Vietnam over the past eight years, a personal journey of reconciliation with the Vietnamese people and, more significantly, a mission of love and mercy to help victims of the war with physical and/or neurological damage resulting from Agent Orange (e.g., blindness, deafness, physical deformities). In doing so, he followed in the footsteps of a unique cohort of fellow Vietnam veterans who—despite scant awareness among the U.S. public—have labored in-country for decades, seeking resolution and healing by helping to heal those Vietnamese still suffering from the terrible legacy of the 20-year conflict.

On his initial visit to Vietnam, Michael was surprised to be met with so much understanding, forgiveness, and optimism from the Vietnamese people. "I was accompanied on that first trip by my younger brother, Mark, who gave me invaluable encouragement and helped to show me how kind and respectful the Vietnamese people were to the US war veterans. My emotional trauma almost disappeared in the first few hours I was there." Michael shook the hands of five former North Vietnamese soldiers. "They were all smiles, one of them said to me, 'peace is good.'" He also encountered two English women who had been activists against the Vietnam War. The women, who interviewed Michael, were working on a documentary about the incredible work being done by former G.I.'s in Vietnam. The documentary, titled "You're the Enemy. Welcome Back," was released shortly thereafter, and has been shown all over the world.

(Note: For more information on the amazing activities of these selfless former G.I.'s in Vietnam, check the internet for "Vietnam Friendship Village Hanoi" or "Project Renew Vietnam.")

The front gates at Friendship Village in Hanoi, Vietnam. The village is a residential facility that provides medical care, physical therapy, education and vocational training to Vietnamese children, young adults and veterans suffering from maladies most likely caused by use of the chemical defoliant Agent Orange.

Michael Gillum meeting with former North Vietnamese regulars at Friendship Village in 2013. These ex-soldiers go to the village for R&R and periodic medical checkups. Photo provided.

CHAPTER 20

John Ashe: Cold War Warrior with the U.S. Air Force

John and his twin brother were born on April 17, 1942, in Suffolk, Virginia. His family soon moved to Newport News, Virginia, where his father worked at the famous Newport News shipyard and, in the early 1950s, became one of the first African-American police officers to serve with the Newport News Police Department. As John recalled: "Newport News is a military community, and I was unaware that I had been predestined to join the military. My home town of Newport News is surrounded by the Navy, Army, Air Force, and Coast Guard, so we were exposed to patriotism in school and daily life. My uncles served in the U.S. Army, the U.S. Coast Guard and [we were near] Langley Air Force Base and the Norfolk naval base where

A recent photograph of John Ashe and his wife, Maria. Photo provided.

aeronautics history was being made."

In 1957, John went on his very first date with a young lady named Rosabelle Jenkins, who had invited him to accompany her to hear a guest speaker at the local Baptist Church. The guest speaker was Dr. Martin Luther King, Jr. In his speech, Dr. King talked about the struggles of black people seeking justice and equal rights; he also opined that, even when confronted with obstacles in life, one should always do the very best that he can at whatever his job in life might be. Dr. King's counsel to always "do your best" has inspired John throughout his life and career.

John graduated from Huntington High School in 1960 with the intention of attending Norfolk State College. Unfortunately, family finances precluded sending John to college, and thus, at the urging of a friend, he joined the Air Force. As John stated proudly, on December 28, 1960, "my service to our great nation began. I departed Newport News for basic training at Lackland Air Force Base, Texas." While in basic, John's aptitude test scores revealed that he was highly qualified in the mechanical field; perforce, he was selected for training at Amarillo Air Force Base, Texas, to become a B-47 "Stratojet" bomber maintenance technician. In May 1961, Airman 3rd Class Ashe was assigned to Pease Air Force Base, New Hampshire, and the 509th Bomb Wing—perhaps the most historic wing in our Air Force for, in August 1945, it had changed the arc of history by dropping atomic bombs on both Hiroshima and Nagasaki, hastening the end of World War II.

At Pease AFB, John recalled his experience working on his first Boeing B-47E bomber: "My crew chief was Harold Bostick, a big tall Texan and I was very intimidated by him; however, he became a key person, trainer/mentor, and a life-long friend. He was a man who did not see skin color. He enabled me to grow and helped me to achieve more out of life and a successful Air Force career than I could ever have imagined." During our discussion, John noted that he "owed a debt of gratitude" to many of his superiors and co-workers at Pease

AFB. "Considering [the state of] race relations in the 1960s, these men treated me like a man, and I came to admire them."

Among John's most memorable experiences as a young Airman

The Boeing B-47 "Stratojet" was a long-range strategic bomber capable of striking targets within the Soviet Union with nuclear weapons.

were the 13-day Cuban Missile Crisis in October 1962, and the assassination of President John F. Kennedy on November 22, 1963. During the Cuban Missile Crisis, the 509th Bomb Wing was placed on full alert, its B-47 bombers loaded with nuclear weapons and flown to a forward operating base for potential launch against targets in the Soviet Union. Following Kennedy's assassination, John, now a crew chief, was placed on alert duty ("we were notified that the President had been assassinated; we were upgraded to a higher alert status with a fully loaded bomber with nuclear weapons ready to be launched") and selected to go TDY for 90 days to Upper Hayford Air Base in the United Kingdom. Indeed, during his time at Pease AFB, from May 1961 to November 1965, John was often selected as one of the youngest Airmen to perform alert duty with a B-47 bomber—fully armed with nuclear weapons and ready to go to war in support of our nation against the Soviet Union.

After leaving Pease AFB, John's Air Force career took him across the globe—e.g., to the Philippines, Guam, Spain, Egypt, Saudi Arabia, the U.K., the Azores, Hawaii (as Senior Enlisted Advisor to the 6594th Test Group), and to several Air Force bases in the continental United States. Between 1966 and 1974, John saw temporary duty in South Vietnam on more than a half-dozen occasions, the TDYs lasting from 90 days to as long as six months. In 1986 he finally landed in the California high desert at Edwards AFB, where he served as the Air Force Flight Test Center Maintenance Superintendent and Maintenance Manager for the B-2 bomber flight test program.

On February 1, 1988, Chief Master Sergeant Ashe retired from the Air Force after 27 years, one month, and four days of honorable military service. His list of medals and commendations is long and impressive and includes the following: Meritorious Service Medal with 3 Oak Leaf Clusters, Air Force Commendation Medal, Air Force Outstanding Unit Award with 3 Oak Leaf Clusters, Air Force Good Conduct Medal with more than 7 Awards, Vietnam Service Medal with Bronze Stars, Air Force Organizational Excellence Award with 2 Oak Leaf Clusters, Republic of Vietnam Gallantry with Palm, Republic of Vietnam Campaign Medal, and U.S. Coast Guard Commendation Medal.

A newly-minted civilian, John went to work for the Northrop Grumman Corporation's B-2 bomber division as an integrated logistics support test and evaluation project manager at both Palmdale and Edwards AFB. He retired from Northrop Grumman on July 1, 1995, and resides with his wife, Maria, in Golden Hills.

When asked how he ended up in the Tehachapi area, he said, "After coming out to Edwards Air Force Base, I became familiar with Tehachapi. I wasn't all that crazy about Lancaster, where I lived for about a year. I drove up to Tehachapi on July 2, 1988, to look around and see what the place was like. I said to myself, 'I could live here!'" I moved to Golden Hills in October 1988 and have been here ever since." John married Maria (his second wife) in April 1995. Together they have raised a blended family.

As our interview concluded, this author asked John, "What would you say to a young person today who is thinking of a career in the military?" To which he responded: "You asked the right guy! I tell young people they should consider the military because it will build character, instill a strong work ethic, teach them a trade, and give them something to build on that will last a lifetime."

John—all of Kern County salutes you for your 27 years, one month, and four days of truly honorable service to our great country!

(Note: After many years of dedicated work, John published a beautiful hardback book in 2020 titled, *509th Bomb Wing Veterans Association. A Collection of Biographies and Memoirs of World War II and Cold War Veterans and Patriots*. The book offers a unique narrative and

This photograph of the 509th Bomb Wing Veterans Association, Whiteman AFB, Missouri, adorns the cover of John's book. The photograph was taken in 2003. Photo Provided.

pictorial history of the wing.)

PART FOUR

From Desert Storm to Iraqi Freedom

CHAPTER 21

Father Wes Clare:
A Life of Service to God & Country

Father Wes Clare has served for almost two decades as Rector of the "Saint Jude's in the Mountains" Anglican Church in Tehachapi. His calling to Saint Jude's was the culmination of a remarkable life of service to God, country, and to hundreds of often broken lives to whom he had ministered over the years. In Tehachapi, in addition to his ministry at Saint Jude's, he served for 17 years as an Air National Guard chaplain.

Father Wes Clare in Iraq. Photo provided.

Wes was born in a little farm town in eastern Washington in 1962. Several years later (1966), his family (Wes had an older brother and sister) moved to Oregon, where his father, a college professor, taught American studies at Linfield College. The family moved again in 1972—this time to Olympia, Washington—where Wes graduated from High School in 1981. On his high school senior trip to Europe, he toured the towering Rheims Cathedral in France. It was a transformative moment for the young man: "Overwhelmed by the sense of God's presence in this holy place, I committed myself to the ministry."

Wes then went off to college at Washington State, where he studied computer science and enrolled in Air Force ROTC. As a freshman, he received a 3½ year ROTC scholarship that covered his tuition and books; in return, Wes signed a four-year Air Force service agreement with the goal of becoming an aircraft navigator. While at Washington State, Wes met Wendy (whom he would marry in July 1989) and also got involved in lay ministry at a nearby church. "While in high school, I had been bullied a lot and told by my peers that I'd never amount to anything. [At college] God brought to my attention other folks whose lives were really chewed up and who needed a friend. The bullying I experienced had made me sensitive to others who also hurt inside." For his senior year, he transferred to Evergreen State College, graduating in August 1985 with a degree in computer science and becoming the only student ever from Evergreen (a very "progressive" college) to graduate from ROTC.

On the day he graduated from college, Wes was commissioned as a 2nd Lieutenant in the U.S. Air Force. Over the next couple of years, he completed navigator flight school ("I got my navigator wings") at Mather AFB, California; electronic warfare (EW) school, where, as an EW officer he was taught to protect the aircraft from enemy fire, radar detection, or any other threat (also at Mather AFB); and B-52 bomber combat crew training at Castle AFB, California (May 1987). Wes loved flying in the venerable B-52 bomber, affectionately called the "BUFF" (I won't spell it out!) by its crew members: "Through my entire flying career, the funniest part was flying at low altitude (500 feet) and scaring the cows in the fields, or flying at high altitude and talking to truckers with the HF radio tuned to the CB channel."

In June 1987, 2nd Lieutenant Clare participated in three weeks of aircrew survival training at Fairchild AFB, Washington state. "That's where I learned to eat insects, hide like a bunny rabbit, and put up

B-52G bombers on the flightline at Wurtsmith AFB, Michigan (n.d.)

with the joys of POW training!" Thereafter, Wes was transferred to Wurtsmith AFB, Missouri, for his first assignment—as EW officer on a B-52G in the 524th Bombardment Squadron ("our mission was nuclear deterrence"). Wes was promoted to captain in 1989.

In August 1990, Iraq's dictator, Saddam Hussein, launched his surprise invasion of Kuwait. The U.S. and Allied nations responded with a massive buildup of air, ground, and naval forces in the Middle East with the objective of undoing Saddam's act of aggression. In the fall of 1990, Captain Clare's aircrew was tasked to take part in Operation Desert Storm. On January 17, 1991, his B-52G, part of a three-ship cell, departed Wurtsmith AFB at 3:00 a.m. in a snowstorm with a full load of weapons (36 CBU-87 cluster bombs) and struck an Iraqi Republican Guards command post on the outskirts of Kuwait City. Recalled Wes: "We slept so soundly after being up for 36 hours on our first mission that I awoke with a crooked neck that stayed that way for three days!"

Based in Jeddah, Saudi Arabia, for the remainder of the war, Wes's B-52 bomber flew a total of 25 combat missions over Iraq and Kuwait, with the last mission taking place on February 28, the final day of the war and the day his and Wendy's first daughter, Stephanie, was born. Looking back, Wes recollected that his biggest mission was as part of an 18-ship B-52 strike package that disgorged 900 bombs on a major Iraqi military base ("wreckage from that strike is still there"). But the most dangerous experience occurred on his third combat mission: "We struck a target, a command center in Iraq, and the Iraqi's were waiting for us! We had to do some very clever flying to avoid getting hit by the 100mm anti-aircraft guns. The bomber behind us was hit by flak, which tore a hole just two feet away from its liquid oxygen, which, if it had been struck, the plane would have exploded in the sky." More philosophically, Wes opined: "Being shot at changes you. But you also become mindful of God's protection. I didn't have PTSD, but I did have combat stress. It didn't control my life, or take away my sleep, but for years I would flinch when I heard the french fry alarm at McDonald's because it sounded just like the missile warning alarm in the jet!"

In March 1991, Wes and his crew returned to Wurtsmith AFB via Fairford Air Base, England. Just outside Fairford is one of England's oldest churches, where it just so happened that Wes's wife Wendy's grandmother had been baptized. "I met folks of that parish and did some ministry with them." When Wes made it back to Wurtsmith, he was surprised by a ticker-tape parade. "I wasn't used to being spoiled. I thought to myself, what's happening here? They were even carrying our luggage for us!" Following Desert Storm, Wes became a tactics instructor with the 379th Bombardment Wing (also at Wurtsmith AFB) for about a year and a half. When he was offered a severance package that covered the cost of seminary school, he hung up his wings in August 1992.

Wes graduated from the Trinity School for Ministry (located outside

Pittsburg) in 1995 with a Master of Divinity degree. Wes and Wendy's son, Warren, was born at this time and, in June 1996, Wes was ordained as a minister. The growing family travelled to Wyoming, where Wes was Vicar at his first parish for about five years; daughters Hannah and Erin were born in 1998 and 2000, respectively, completing the Clare family.

In September 2002, the Clare family finally arrived in Tehachapi, with Father Wes becoming the Rector of Saint Jude's in the Mountains Anglican Church. Or as he put it, "in Tehachapi they needed a priest who could talk 'airplane,' as many folks worked in the aviation world. So it's been a perfect fit ever since."

Commissioned as a chaplain in the Air National Guard (June 2002), Father Wes ministered to the 119th Fighter Wing, stationed in Fargo, North Dakota (a two-year stint). At Fargo, he provided pastoral care to F-16 fighter pilots who had launched out of Langley AFB, Virginia, to shoot down Flight 93 during the terror attacks on September 11, 2001. While these fighter pilots were en route to intercept Flight 93, which seemed to be on its way to strike the capitol building in Washington D.C., it crashed in a field in Pennsylvania due to the remarkable resistance put up by the plane's passengers.

In 2005, Father Wes joined the 144th Fighter Wing in Fresno (California National Guard) and that fall deployed as a Guard chaplain to provide pastoral care for soldiers and those affected by Hurricane Katrina (he was embedded with an Army National Guard battalion on this deployment). In 2009, he was off to Balad Air Base, Iraq, where he was assigned to the 332nd Air Expeditionary Wing. "We worked with lots of wounded. Some of them had severe trauma to their bodies. We were able to rescue 12 marriages and stop a handful of suicides during that [Guard] deployment. When those faces of the wounded and the dying, those ghosts if you will, come to mind, they're no longer unwelcome to me. I see it as God reminding me to pray for their families, so I'm grateful for that painful experience."

In 2013, Father Wes was selected as State Chaplain for the California National Guard, placing him in charge of the entire California Air and Army National Guard Chaplain Corps. Promoted to Colonel in the Guard in 2015, he continued as State Chaplain until his retirement from the Guard in March 2020. During his final years as State Chaplain, he made sure that all National Guard units "spun up" to work on the fires in California had their chaplains at their side; the pastoral care these chaplains provided saved marriages and dramatically reduced suicides, until in 2019 and 2020 there were no suicides to report.

Father Wes: As Johann Wolfgang von Goethe once opined, "To think is easy. To act is hard. But the hardest thing in the world is to act in accordance with your thinking." You, Sir, embody Goethe's truism, for you have always thought about putting others before yourself, about protecting your community and your country; yet unlike the vast multitudes, you have consistently acted on those noble thoughts. We honor and we salute you, Father Wes, for a noble life, well-led, in service of others.

CHAPTER 22

Tracey Keefe: Anti-Submarine Warfare Helicopter Pilot in Persian Gulf

Tracey Keefe (née Alexander) was born and grew up in Massachusetts. Her parents owned and operated a small school bus company. "They were really awesome people," Tracey said. "My parents doing that business, particularly in the winter, taught me a lot about determination and fortitude, about doing the right thing every day." Tracey attended grade school and high school in a town situated just outside Boston. In high school, she ran track (50 and 100-yard hurdles) and was a member of the drama club, in which she had a couple of lead roles in plays. "The drama club helped me learn to do public speaking, to talk to people. I had no idea how helpful that would be later in life."

Tracey Keefe in the cockpit of her helicopter. Photo provided.

Tracey enrolled at Boston University, where she earned a BA in geology. About midway through college, she became interested in joining the U.S. Navy. Like so many adventuresome youths before her, she wanted to join the Navy and see the world! "I applied for and was accepted by Navy ROTC," she said. "I went to college in the late 1980s and early 1990s, and I really wanted to have a good job after college. And ever since I was a young child, I've loved to travel. So Navy aviation seemed like a really good idea to me."

After graduating from Navy ROTC—and much to her delight—she received her commission as an ensign (a commissioned rank in the Navy or Coast Guard that is below lieutenant junior grade) next to the historic USS Constitution, one of the six original frigates authorized under the Naval Act of 1794, and a warship that had played a major role in the Barbary Wars, the War of 1812, and in defending sea lanes until 1855.

In the spring of 1991, the newly-minted ensign was assigned to a helicopter squadron at Norfolk Naval Air Station (NAS), Virginia. In March 1992, she began flight training at Pensacola NAS, Florida; however, the "flight training" at Pensacola—where she spent two months—wasn't what one might typically consider flight training at all; rather, it was the tough physical conditioning that preceded actual hands-on flight training (in addition to some aviation-related academics). "It was really intense. We did the obstacle course; lots of running in the sand; lots of aquatic survival training, such as swimming long distances and swimming with our gear on. We also did simulated aircraft underwater egress training."

Tracey performed her primary (basic) flight training course in Corpus Christi, Texas, from May to December 1992. She and the other pilot trainees in her class all flew the Beechcraft T-34, a single-engine, two-seat turboprop (propeller-driven) basic trainer, which Tracey described as "really powerful for a trainer aircraft." After basic flight training, she returned to Florida—this time for advanced flight training at Whiting Field (close to Pensacola NAS). At Whiting, she began to fly the Bell TH-57C helicopter. "I really fell in love with helicopters. I loved flying closer to the ground. The helicopter fit me like a glove [she is only 5' 2"], the cockpit was quite comfortable for me. And I really loved those I worked with in the helicopter community. I look back, and I still think of the wonderful people with whom I served."

She received her flight "wings" in September 1993. "That was a great day. My family came out from Massachusetts to be present. And this was when it became interesting." It became interesting because the military had only recently lifted the combat exclusion for women. While Tracey was aware of this historic change, "it was more of an afterthought. In the back of my mind, I believed that the lifting [of the exclusion] wouldn't apply to [my training class]. Yet to her surprise, she soon found herself assigned to a major combat unit—Helicopter Anti-Submarine Squadron 6 (HS-6) at NAS North Island in San Diego.

Yet upon arriving at North Island, her initial assignment was with Helicopter Anti-Submarine Squadron 10 (HS-10), whose mission was to train pilots and aircrew in carrier-based rotary wing anti-submarine warfare (ASW). Of course, in the early 1990s, few women were serving as pilots of any kind in the U.S. military, so her arrival at North Island raised more than a few eyebrows. "I'll never forget. I showed up at North Island with my orders, and the squadron training officer looked at me and said, 'Hmmm, I guess we'll have to notify the commander. He [the training officer] was clearly surprised that I was a woman. Speaking to the commander, he said, 'I have Lieutenant Alexander in my office, and *she*. . ." Yet no matter, for Tracey was "thrilled" to be stationed on the west coast. "I was thinking, 'this is great, I've won the lottery.'" Indeed, the west coast was attractive to Tracey for several reasons, not least of which was that her Marine helicopter pilot boyfriend was about to be stationed on the west coast as well.

While serving with HS-10, Tracey trained on the Sikorsky SH-60 "Seahawk," a twin turboshaft engine, multi-mission Navy helicopter based on the Army's UH-60 Black Hawk. In January 1995, she joined HS-6, which at that time was operating as part of Carrier Air Wing 11 from the deck of the nuclear aircraft carrier USS Abraham Lincoln. During her three-year stint with HS-6, Tracey experienced two major deployments to the Persian Gulf (the second aboard the carrier USS Kitty Hawk). All told, she spent 16 months at sea, flying missions to enforce the no-fly zone against Iraq, ASW missions, and, most of all, search and rescue missions.

During her first deployment—which was only the second time that women had been permanently assigned to a carrier air wing—night

Tracey Keefe and her young sons. Photo provided.

vision goggles were not yet in common use in the Navy, so she had to do a lot of instrument flying, often barely 200 feet above the gulf. "Flying at night over water could be difficult, but I was blessed never to have been involved in any direct combat operations. I was never actually shot at. And, once again, I was treated wonderfully. I found a good deal of camaraderie in the helicopter community." Between deployments, in 1996, Tracey married her Marine helicopter fiancé, Ed Keefe, who has since flown combat missions on subsequent deployments to Iraq.

In January 1998, Tracey was selected to teach a leadership course at the Navy Leader Training Unit, Naval Amphibious Base, Coronado, California. Teaching turned out to be a "great experience" for her; among other things, it enabled her to travel throughout the continental United States. She resigned from active duty in late 2000. About the same time, Tracey gave birth to her first son; a second son was born to the Keefe family in 2002.

Yet Tracey's commitment to the Navy did not end when she left active service. For more than a decade thereafter (2000-2011), she was in the Naval Reserve. While in the Reserve, she supported aircraft and weapons acquisition and various test programs. Throughout this period, she was primarily assigned to Naval Air Weapons Station, China Lake, California, while also seeing stints at NAS Point Mugu, California, and NAS Patuxent River, Maryland. Working with a combination of very sharp aviators and engineers at first posed a somewhat daunting challenge to Tracey. "Most of the time, I was working with people who were a lot smarter than I am. But it was a great experience. I was so in over my head. For the first few years, I didn't want to open my mouth! I eventually became the executive officer for my detachment, so I had to get over that."

Presently, she is employed in a human rcsources position in Tehachapi for World Wind & Solar, a company in the field of renewable energy.

As our interview neared its end, Tracey made it clear that she still had something she needed to convey, something very important to her. This is what she said: "Of all the interesting and challenging jobs I've had, I feel that being a good parent was really the most important and most difficult. You only have one chance to get it right. I didn't start out as a natural mother. I had to go from being a Navy pilot to being a mother—that was the biggest challenge of all. The two boys are young adults now, both in college and in Army ROTC. So the effort certainly paid off."

Tracey—I know your two sons and can confirm that all your efforts as a mother paid off, and handsomely so! We in Kern County honor you and your husband Ed, for shepherding two fine young men into adulthood and, just as importantly, we honor both of you for such selfless service to our country.

CHAPTER 23

Adam Zanutto: American Hero Killed by Roadside Bomb in Ramadi, Iraq

Adam was born on November 6, 1979, in Bakersfield to Richard ("Rick") and Donna Zanutto. He spent most of his much-too-short life in Walker Basin, a valley in the Southern Sierra Nevada with magnificent scenery and spectacular sunsets that locals long ago had christened "God's Country." More specifically, he grew up outside Bakersfield in the town of Caliente, a ranching and farming community where his father had a hay farming business

Adam Zanutto in his Marine Dress Uniform. Photo provided.

Adam attended Piute Mountain School in Twin Oaks from Kindergarten through the eighth grade. The tiny school—just 100 or so students and five classrooms in Adam's time there—is quite unique, as it was built largely underground (in the early 1980s) in an effort to make it more energy efficient; only the south-facing windows, with a breathtaking view of the mountains, are discernable from the outside. Of course, the playground is above ground, and today is named in honor of Adam ("Adam's Playground"). His mother worked at the school for 25 years as a librarian and paraprofessional (teacher's aide).

"When Adam came home from school, he'd move sprinklers in the alfalfa fields, or he'd rake hay," his father recalled. "He was always working with me on the farm. No matter what I asked him to do, he never complained, he always did what needed to be done, and I think that's one reason he was such a good Marine."

As a youngster, Adam played AYSO soccer and Little League Baseball in Lake Isabella, even pitching a no-hitter on one occasion. "His coach gave him the game ball, and we still have it after all these years," his father said.

His love of sports, leadership skills, and competitive drive were also evident at Foothill High School in Bakersfield, where he played soccer and one year of football. On his high school soccer team all four years, Adam would unselfishly dish out assists to his teammates. In fact, he was happier to assist on a game-winning goal than he was to score it.

After graduating from high school in 1998, Adam attended Bakersfield College, where he took classes in criminal justice that would help to mold his desire to serve his country. Adam always evinced a love of our country's history and its many sacrifices for freedom—convictions shaped in part by watching the History Channel and iconic films such as the "Sands of Iwo Jima," "Black Hawk Down," and "Band of Brothers."

The tragic events of September 11, 2001, deeply affected Adam and strengthened his eagerness to serve. In October 2002, he enlisted in the Marine Corps; he did so not only to support his country, to protect our freedoms, but to honor his family's tradition of military service.

"It was almost like a calling for Adam. He had cousins and uncles who had fought in World War II, Korea, and Vietnam," his father, a Vietnam veteran, explained. "He was intrigued by my experiences in Vietnam. He would see my [Army] uniform hanging in the closet, look at my photographs. And he really took an interest after 9/11. Adam was a very quiet person, he didn't talk much, but that day clearly had a tremendous impact on him. He put his dreams and his aspirations on hold to [enlist] in the Marine Corps. It's as if he felt compelled in some way to do so."

Adam went through basic training at Camp Pendleton, one of the

Adam (L) in Iraq. Photo provided.

largest Marine Corps bases in the U.S., on the coast of Southern California (San Diego County). After basic, he took his Advanced Infantry Training (AIT), also at Camp Pendleton, selecting the Military Occupational Specialty (MOS) of infantry machine gunner. He was then transferred to the Marine Corps base at Twentynine Palms in the Southern California desert. Here he joined the 3rd Battalion, 7th Marine Regiment, Ist Marine Division, I Marine Expeditionary Force.

Operation Iraqi Freedom began on March 19, 2003, with preemptive airstrikes on Saddam Hussein's Presidential Palace and key military targets. Iraqi ground forces were rapidly overwhelmed, and Baghdad seized barely five weeks later. Yet what at first appeared to be a brilliant success for U.S. arms, soon deteriorated into a protracted insurgency, as al Qaeda fighters poured into the country and unleashed a tenacious guerilla war.

Corporal Zanutto would see three tours of duty in Iraq. His first tour (2003) took him to Karbala and was of seven months' duration. After returning home for a short period of leave, he soon found himself back to Iraq—this time (2004) at Al Quim, near the Syrian border, where his regiment sought to prevent the infiltration of al Qaeda fighters into Iraq. His third tour (2005/06) was in Ramadi, west of Baghdad, in Al Anbar province, a hotbed of terrorist activity. On July 4, 2005, shortly before returning again to Iraq, Adam had tied the knot with his sweetheart, Amber.

In addition to training as a combat infantryman, Adam had earned his Emergency Medical Technician (EMT) certificate in the Marine Corps and, on January 5, 2006, he put those skills to good use, assisting in a mass casualty evacuation at a glass factory in Ramadi where a suicide bomb attack had killed or wounded over 100 Iraqi civilians. For his actions, he was awarded the Navy and Marine Corps Achievement Medal.

Adam was now a Marine squad leader, a tribute to his knowledge and leadership skills. He and his men were often out on patrol, and as many of his fellow Marines would later attest, he had a way of calming their anxieties before a mission. He approached his responsibilities with the utmost seriousness and preparation; indeed, before beginning his tour in Ramadi, while still at home between tours, he and his father had gone to a Kinko's print shop in Bakersfield to have some maps of the terrain in Al Anbar province printed and laminated. Adam wanted to study the terrain before his deployment; he also wanted to have maps at his disposal that would hold up better—better than those provided by the Marine Corps—under the harsh conditions in the Iraqi desert.

On February 23, 2006, Adam sent an email to his parents. He was eager, he said, to return home to his parents and his new family (his wife had two children). He noted enthusiastically that he only had 27 days left in Iraq.

Two days later, February 25th, Adam and his squad were out on patrol in Ramadi. One of the lightly armored, four-wheel drive military vehicles—colloquially known as "Humvee's"—in his column suffered a mechanical breakdown, forcing Adam's Humvee to turn around to check out the problem. At some point, his vehicle struck a roadside bomb. Adam was severely wounded and flown back to the National Naval Medical Center in Bethesda, Maryland, where he died of his wounds on March 6th, with his wife and mother at his side. Adam, 26, was laid to rest at Hillcrest Memorial Park in Bakersfield. He was one of nearly 4500 U.S. servicemen and women to die in the Iraq war through 2019. (Note: Adam was posthumously awarded his sergeant's strips by the Marine Corps (he had studied for, and passed, the sergeant's test)).

Another photograph of Adam in Iraq. Photo provided.

That Adam was respected, even loved, by the Marines who served with him is underscored in these heartfelt remarks of Sgt. Judson:

"I wasn't gonna do this, but I can't let it go, I miss this guy so much. If anybody reads this, these are some things they should know about him. Adam . . . first of a great man, a great man makes a great Marine. His sense of humor, his personality . . . just a great guy. He took care of the guys beneath him and trained them the best he could, stern but approachable. The day I saw him in pain will never leave me, and I've been in pain ever since. It hurts to lose somebody but a friend and a leader is even worse. My heart goes out to his love and his family. He was everything I want to be and more, and I miss him every day. My deepest condolences and sorrow." (http://fallenheroesmemorial.com)

Adam had been scheduled to be discharged from the Marines in October 2006 (his wife, Amber, had moved to Bakersfield to prepare for his return). His career aspiration was to become a Kern County Sheriff's deputy.

An American flag had flown outside the Zanuttos' family home all of Adam's life. "If I'd miss a day, he would be out there to put it up," his father said. The day Adam died, he said, "the hardest thing for me to do in my life was lower that flag."

In 2007, Rick and Donna Zanutto moved to Tehachapi, the result of Rick's decision to finally retire. (Rick's brother and his wife were already living in Tehachapi.) Rick had been publisher of a periodical called "The Fence Post," which covers Kern County history, so he and his wife knew the Tehachapi area well.

On October 7, 2020, the Major Jason E. George VFW presented a Gold Star to Rick Zanutto, for the loss of his son Adam in Iraq.

(Note: A portrait of Adam, resplendent in his Marine Corps dress uniform, painted by Thomas Zachery, hangs proudly in the Portrait of a Warrior Gallery in Bakersfield. It was the very first portrait painted for the gallery.)

CHAPTER 24

Jason E. George: American Hero Killed by IED in Baghdad, Iraq

"For the whole earth is the tomb of famous men; not only are they commemorated by columns and inscriptions, but there dwells also an unwritten memorial of them, graven not on stone but in the hearts of men." Pericles Funeral Oration (ca. 431 BC)

Jason George at West Point. Photo provided.

Jason Everett George was born in Bakersfield on November 3, 1971, the son of Hugh and Candace Mason (Jason's biological father was Clyde George). "JG" grew up in the high desert of California. He was passionate about the Los Angeles Dodgers and American automobiles, while one of his amusing idiosyncrasies was wearing shorts, even in the coldest climates. Jason was one of those rare souls with rcal charisma, remembered for his "great smile and a charming and endearing personality that was a big hit with everyone, including members of the fairer sex."

At Tehachapi High School, Jason played a variety of competitive sports, kicking the winning field goal in the finals of the Desert Inyo League Championships his senior year. He graduated in 1988 as salutatorian (second highest academic rank in his class). By this time in his young life he had also become an Eagle Scout, had worked for NASA, played in a marching band, and been elected president of his National Honor Society. Jason, in fact, had become the "all-American boy!"

After high school, Jason enrolled at California State University Bakersfield, immersing himself in the academic, social, and political activities of the college. He served as social chairman of the Sigma Pi Fraternity, intramural sports chairman, and vice president of the Inter-Fraternity Council, while also finding time to be active with the University Republicans Club and the (no doubt) lesser known Scholastic Surfing Association.

After a year of study at California State, Jason received a prestigious appointment to the West Point Military Academy (he had also been accepted by the Navy and Air Force academies!), eventually graduating second in his class of about 1400 cadets. In 1994, he was commissioned as a second lieutenant in the Army and, as was his wont, he fearlessly tackled the many new challenges at hand. Serving eight years as a combat engineer, he earned his Ranger tab, became a distinguished graduate of the Armor Officers Advanced Course, and deployed to Bosnia, before finally being stationed in Savannah, Georgia.

Jason left active duty in 2002 and enrolled at the University of Michigan Business School, where he earned an MBA. Again, while at Ann Arbor, he was extremely active, playing for the UMBS Rugby Club and, inter alia, serving as an admissions ambassador and the fundraising chair for the Go Blue Rendezvous (an event hosted by the business school for incoming MBA students). After receiving his

MBA, Jason moved to Chicago, where he worked as a healthcare consultant. At the time, he was also in the Army Reserve, meeting his drilling obligations serving as a liaison for the West Point admissions office.

In early 2009, Jason was recalled to active duty and assigned to the 1-252nd Combined Arms Battalion in Iraq. As a friend recalled, Jason might have been able to use his Reserve duty at West Point to "pull strings" to avoid duty in Iraq. "A lot of guys would fight it or hire a lawyer to get out of it, but he didn't. He said, 'This is my duty, and I'm gonna go.' He had no hesitation, which is a real tribute to how he felt about his country."

Indeed, Jason did not shrink from his nation's call but stepped forward boldly to embrace it. He flew into Kuwait on April 22, 2009, and reached his destination, Baghdad, by May 5th. In the war-torn Iraqi capital, Jason was assigned one of the most challenging tasks an American soldier could ever be given—to help the Iraqi people stand on their own. His mission was to help revitalize the Iraqi economy—e.g., by promoting electricity generation, water, education, and health

A Memorial service in Iraq for Major Jason George, 1st Lt. Leevi Barnard, and Sgt. Paul Brooks. Photo provided.

care—while his brothers in arms continued to target and eliminate the enemy networks that were terrorizing the Iraqi people and Coalition Forces.

On the fateful morning of May 21, 2009, Major George and supporting military personnel planned to meet near an outdoor market in southern Baghdad with the leadership of the Dora Market Businessmen's Association to discuss the ongoing revitalization of the local business community. As the U.S. soldiers entered the appointed building, they were suddenly attacked by a terrorist outfitted with an improvised explosive device (IED) suicide vest. In the ensuing blast, Jason, 38 years old, lost his life along with two national guardsmen, 1st Lt. Leevi K. Barnard (28, of Mount Airy, North Carolina), and Sgt. Paul F. Brooks (34, of Joplin, Missouri); other soldiers were seriously wounded, while a number of innocent Iraqi civilians were killed and injured

Because Jason E. George had touched so many lives in such meaningful ways, his death elicited an outpouring of grief in local newspapers (including the Los Angeles Times) and on social media. These included the following:

- "Jason was a man in full. His honor, intelligence, competitiveness, loyalty, and humor are unmatched. The United States has given one of its best with his passing. May God bless and comfort his family, friends, and fellow soldiers. Rest in Peace, Jason." (Justin Gernot)

- "I fell in love with Jason when my family and I met him on the day we took our son Spencer to West Point. I watched JG grow into a truly kind, considerate, and totally genuine young man in those next four years, and then afterwards into a fine and capable [Marine] officer. . . He was a universal man and a good friend to so many who will now sorely miss his presence on this earthly plane. Heaven has indeed gained a new star . . . and I shall treasure the thought of seeing him again there one day." (Sherry Kympton)

- "I am deeply saddened that such a beautiful man, inside and out, has been taken from our grasp. God Bless you, Jason. Your commitment to service is why I am able to see my children and family every day. Words cannot express my gratitude. Your beautiful smile, your commitment, will never be forgotten." (Julie Benz Sanchez)

Jason always sent both his mother and grandmother flowers on Mother's Day. And he worried about his terminally ill grandfather. In his final e-mail from Iraq, he asked if he could make a call to the doctors who were in charge of his grandfather's care. He ended every call with, "I love you, Mom. I love you, Dad."

Jason was the first of his West Point class to die in direct combat. He was also the first person to be buried at the Bakersfield National Cemetery. His awards include: the Meritorious Service Medal, Army Commendation Medal, Army Achievement Medal, two National Defense Medals, Army Service Medal, and Iraq Campaign Medal with Bronze Service Star, as well as posthumous Bronze Star and Purple Heart Medals.

Jason George's burial plot. He was the first to be buried at the Bakersfield National Cemetery. Photo provided.

Notes: For more about Jason, please consult the Jason George Memorial Foundation, a 501(c)(3) organization "founded to honor the memory and values of Major Jason George" by supporting veterans, promoting civic service, and providing scholarships to those who serve (web site: https://jgf.clubexpress.com).

Local veterans are invited to join VFW Post 12114, founded in Tehachapi by five veterans in honor of Major George. Alex Athans is the current Quarter Master; the post's phone number and web site: 661.979.4250, https://tehachapivfw.org.

CHAPTER 25

Alberto Garcia, Jr.: American Hero Killed by Roadside Bomb in Baghdad, Iraq

Alberto was born on March 9, 1984, in Delano, California. He grew up in Bakersfield, raised by a single mom (Maria Garcia). Alberto was the youngest of three children, having two older sisters, Mercedes and Veronica He attended Vista West High School in Bakersfield, a satellite institution of South High School. While Albert didn't participate in sports formally in high school, he loved baseball and was a big fan of the World Wrestling Federation. He particularly liked the "Rock" (for those who don't know, Dwayne

Alberto Garcia, Jr., proud soldier of the "Big Red One." Photo provided.

Johnson, a.k.a. the "Rock," was a wrestler before he became a mega-star actor), and was so enthusiastic about the WWF that he even got his mother watching the matches! When asked what she remembered most about her son's high school years, Maria replied without hesitation: "He got along with everyone. He was always helping people. He had lots of friends in high school. Whenever I picked him up from school, he was always surrounded by his friends. They called him 'Malachi' in high school—a biblical name that was an expression of Alberto's religious faith." (Malachi: "messenger or angel, the last of the minor prophets, and the writer of the last book of the Old Testament canon," https://www.biblestudytools.com.)

Alberto's many interests included tattoos, hot rods, motorcycles, comic books, punk rock and, not to be overlooked, he was a huge fan of Johnny Cash. He was an active member of the Valley Bible Fellowship Church, often patrolling church grounds, praying, and ministering to others. He kept his love of the Lord at the center of his life. In the military, on his "MySpace" page, two of the people that he said he'd like to meet someday were God and, you guessed it, Johnny Cash.

As Maria explained, her son also loved all things military and was determined to join the Army. Indeed, he was a patriot who had always wanted to serve his country as a soldier. When his mother said, "but, Alberto, we are at war [in Afghanistan and Iraq]; you could be killed!" he replied, in his gentle but firm manner, "but mom, I could be killed anywhere at any time. I need to do this." In fact, time and again, he would tell his mother and his sisters, "I need to do this." While he never explained exactly what those five words meant, his mother knew: Alberto was expressing his deep love for God and his country.

Alberto enlisted in the Army on July 26, 2005 (he had worked hard to achieve the ideal weight and to pass the testing required to join the Army). He graduated from One Station Unit Training as an 11B Infantryman assigned to "G" Company, 1st Battalion, 19th Infantry, at Fort Benning, Georgia. He was then assigned to "C" Company

"Rock," 1st Battalion, 26th Infantry (the "Blue Spaders"), 1st Infantry Division, in Schweinfurt, Germany. The 1st Infantry Division (the "Big Red One") was an elite formation—a combined arms division that is the oldest continuously serving division of the Regular Army, having seen continuous service since its organization in 1917 during World War I (it had landed at Omaha Beach in Normandy, France, on June 6, 1944).

Alberto arrived in Germany in early December 2005. Yet with America

SPC Garcia (L) in Iraq with other soldiers of his platoon. Photo provided.

at war with al Qaeda terrorists (and other assorted miscreants) in Iraq, he was only too aware that it wouldn't be long until he and his unit were also in combat there; and, on August 4, 2006, Specialist Garcia ("Specialist" is a junior-enlisted rank) and the "Blue Spaders" deployed in support of Operation Iraqi Freedom.

In Iraq, Alberto—or "Berto," as he was affectionately known to the other soldiers in 1st Platoon, "C" Company—took part in numerous combat patrols in Adamiyah (eastern Baghdad) in support of Operation Together Forward II and the Baghdad Security Plan. He was a dedicated soldier, who "displayed unwavering courage and commitment to his unit and the United States Army." (Task Force 1-26 Infantry, Memorial Ceremony, 20 March 2007, SPC Alberto Garcia, Jr.). Always the dutiful son, during his service in Iraq he kept in close touch with his mother, often sending her money.

On March 13, 2007, while conducting combined security operations in Baghdad, his platoon was struck by enemy small arms fire. In the ensuing combat action, Alberto lost his life as a result of fatal wounds caused by the detonation of an improvised explosive device (IED). He was 23 years old.

At his memorial ceremony in Iraq on March 20, 2007, fellow soldiers of Task Force 1-26 Infantry ("Blue Spaders") poured out their love and respect for Alberto. Some of their remarks are noted below:

LTC Schacht (Battalion Commander):

"He was tall, soft-spoken, and a devout Christian. He loved God and his family and was not embarrassed to publicly display his love for both. Like many Soldiers, Alberto fancied tattoos. He was very proud of his first tattoo, which was an image of Christ. . .

"The Soldiers of Task Force Blue Spaders are fighting in a very difficult and unforgiving sector of Baghdad, and the Soldiers of Charlie 'Rock' Company know this all too well. This past month marks over 7 months of combat service in Northeast Baghdad and our fight in Adhamiyah has been marked by emotional highs and lows. Charlie 'Rock' has been especially successful in capturing numerous high value targets, and the discovery of weapons caches. However, they also know all too well the pain associated with losing a fellow comrade to a shameless enemy. . . Alberto was the sixth soldier lost from this great company. . . Alberto was scheduled to fly home next month to see his family for a long awaited R&R [rest and relaxation]."

CPT Strickland (Company Commander):

"SPC Garcia was an integral part of 1st Platoon. His sense of humor entertained us, his positive attitude motivated us, his Soldiering impressed us, and his faith inspired us. . .

"Almost everyone I've talked to in 1st Platoon said the same thing about Alberto. They said 'Berto' was loved by everyone. . . He was one of those quiet guys who'd not really talk to you until he got to know you, but once he did and he opened up to you, you'd discover a guy that was funny and caring and grounded in his faith in the Lord. You could always count on his for anything. . .

"As a Leader, you couldn't ask for a better Soldier than SPC Garcia. He was disciplined, reliable, quick to learn, aggressive, tough, and never complained. He'd come off a long patrol, and while other guys were starting to relax, Garcia would be squaring his gear away, preparing himself to roll out on the next mission. And when he was done squaring his gear away, he'd hit the gym to square his body away, even if it was 3 in the morning. When I assumed command of Charlie Company, one of the things that I told them that was important to me was Soldiers living the Warrior Ethos. Specialist Alberto Garcia, Jr. WAS the Warrior Ethos. He always placed the mission first; he never quit; he never accepted defeat, and he never left a fellow Soldier in a time of need."

SGT Richardson (Squad Commander):

"I was extremely fortunate to have SPC Alberto Garcia as a member of my squad. He was a soldier that made an NCO's job a little easier. He was a very dependable and loyal Soldier. Alberto loved the physical part of being a Soldier. You could always find him at the gym late at night. He never complained about how tired he was. He was a Soldier who just kept going. . . He always made everything easier for everyone.

"He was a fast learner, and he enjoyed learning as much as he could. He also loved to play his guitar. Although he just started a few months ago, for a beginner, he played extremely well. I remember showing him some basic chords, and the next thing I knew, he was teaching me some Johnny Cash songs." (Task Force 1-26 Infantry, Memorial Ceremony, 20 March 2007, SPC Alberto Garcia, Jr.)

When Captain Strickland went through SPC Garcia's personal belongings, he found a small pocket-size bible stained with Alberto's blood, as well as a piece of paper with several references from Scripture. One of the references was to Psalm 71:1-8, which includes the words: "In you, O Lord, I have taken refuge; let me never be put to shame. Rescue me and deliver me in your righteousness; turn your ear to me and save me. Be my rock of refuge, to which I can always go; give the command to save me, for you are my rock and my fortress. . . I will ever praise you."

The loss of SPC Garcia motivated his band of brothers in "C" Company to search out, kill, and capture those responsible for his death. At 8:30 a.m., the next morning, 2nd Platoon located a suspicious house with a secret room containing several anti-tank mines, over

The hearse bearing SPC Garcia's remains at his funeral. Photo provided.

300 gallons of nitric acid, and more than 125 pounds of homemade explosives. Although the insurgents who had prepared this "recipe for destruction" were nowhere to be found, the platoon provided security for an explosive ordnance disposal team that destroyed the house in a controlled demolition—not only avenging Alberto's death but most likely saving the lives of other members of his company.

SPC Garcia was laid to rest at Hillcrest Memorial Park, on its "Hill of Valor," in Bakersfield. Among his awards and decorations were the following: the Bronze Star Medal, Purple Heart, National Defense Service Medal, Iraqi Campaign Medal, Global War on Terrorism Service Medal, Army Service Ribbon, Overseas Service Ribbon, Drivers Badge, and the Combat Infantryman Badge.

APPENDIX 1:

The Charles B. Burdick Military History Project

(Director, Dr. Jonathan Roth)
(San Jose State University)

The Burdick Project is named after Professor Charles B. Burdick, to honor his memory and his contribution to the study of military history. Charles Burdick graduated as a history major from San Jose State College in 1949, after previously serving in the United States Army. He later went on to pursue his Ph.D. at Stanford University, and his dissertation research on the German High Command in World War II, involved interviews with many of the surviving members of the German General Staff. In 1957, Burdick returned to San Jose State as a member of the History Department, and in 1976, became its chair. He worked to create a vigorous military history program at SJSU and helped build up the library's collection into one of the best on the west coast. During his career, he published dozens of articles and book chapters, and wrote or edited over 20 books. After an association with San Jose State that spanned 45 years, Dr. Burdick retired in 1988. He died in 1998, and in that year, the Project was named in his honor. (source: https://www.facebook.com/burdickhistoryproject).

The Project has sponsored numerous lectures, panels, and talks, including the annual Charles Burdick Memorial Military History Symposium, held every spring since 1996. Topics have included African-Americans in the Military, Women in the Military, the Military History of Iraq, SJSU at War; and our most recent event, a panel discussion "Writing Military History," which included four local writers of popular military history. We also sponsor the annual Harry Gailey Memorial Lecture on a military campaign, as well as other presentations. We also provide support for the Air Force and Army ROTC, military recruiters, and the SJSU Veterans Student Organization. We have donated material for a number of university exhibits, including the 150th anniversary and a recent one in Special Collections on World War II posters.

The Project is located in Industrial Studies, 239 where we keep our collection of more than 5,000 books, journals, pamphlets, field manuals, photographs and artifacts. There is not only an excellent collection of general military history works but many that are quite unusual and even rare. Our American Civil War collection is derived mainly from the personal one of the former State Librarian of Illinois. We have a small collection of donated militaria, including an 1812 Brown Bess musket (kept in the University Police firearms locker) and a 17th century English cavalry helmet. The Project includes a veterans' oral history project, and has collected dozens of oral histories, including those made with a number of faculty veterans.

The Burdick Military History Project Office is open Monday through Friday, 10am to 4pm.

Get Involved: To make donations, volunteer, or join our mailing list, please contact Dr. Jonathan Roth by calling 408.924.5505 or emailing him at jonathan.roth@sjsu.edu.

A portion of the 10,000 books, photographs and artifacts kept in the Burdick Military History Project Collection. Photo provided.

Appendix 2:

Major Jason E. George VFW Post 12114
(Tehachapi, CA)

Major Jason E. George was killed in Iraq in May 2009 (see his story above). As one who knew him well recalled shortly after Jason's passing: "Jason was a man in full. His honor, intelligence, competitiveness, loyalty, and humor are unmatched. The United States has given one of its best with his passing. . . Rest in Peace, Jason."

VFW Post 12114 was established in October 2012 in Tehachapi by veterans Alex Athans, Bill Jasper, Daryl Black, Roger Rolin, Jerry Saville, Larry Hoose. As of late 2021, the post boasted 50 members. Jason's mother was elated to have the post named after her son. "Now he will live forever," she said.

The post is dedicated to connecting veterans of all generations. If you have questions about the benefits you have earned, or you are wanting to connect with other individuals who understand what it is like trying to fit back into civilian society, contact us! We are on a mission to assist young veterans by providing the information you need, and the camaraderie you've been missing.

Major Jason E. George VFW Post 12114 issued a check in the amount of $16,025 to Pancreatic Cancer Action Network In October of 2019, and will continue to raise funds annually. Thank you for your support in the battle against Pancreatic Cancer.

Contact Information: (661) 979-4250 / Quarter Master, Alex Athans.

Jason E. George's West Point ceremonial sword. Photo provided.

Appendix 3:

Portrait of a Warrior Gallery
(Bakersfield, CA)

Memorial Art Gallery featuring the portraits of 27 post 9/11 KIA Fallen Heroes from Kern County. Also the Vietnam Room. Coming Soon 82,000 personalized dog tags recognizing ALL MIAs from WWII to the present.

Mission: To honor and recognize all post 9/11 fallen war heroes from Kern County that were killed in action or as a result of wounds suffered on the battlefield. The Gallery is a gathering place for numerous veterans' organizations, classes, or for simply "hanging out" to bond as brothers and sisters.

"Every inch of this Gallery is designed to honor our Veterans and those serving in our military. The Warrior Gallery showcases our post 9/11 Kern County fallen heroes not only in uniform, but the artists have also painted snapshots from their lives as children on into adulthood. I really liked seeing some additional pieces of memorabilia that shed a bit more light on the lives of these warriors. Our guide introduced us to each service member via their portrait, told us something about their military service and also something personal about them. There are several more rooms and displays at the Gallery. Do not miss the powerfully emotional 22 A Day Wall dedicated to making the public more aware of the suicide rate of veterans and military.” (posted on Facebook by Sandi Jantz)

Location: 1925 Eye Street, Bakersfield, 93301.

Web Site: https://www.facebook.com/PortraitofaWarriorKernCounty

Note: The Gallery is a non-profit, 503c organization.

Some of the marvelous portraits inside the gallery. Photo provided.

Appendix 4:

Fallen Warriors:

Kern County Heroes Honored at Portrait of a Warrior Gallery

(Note: This is a list of all 27 Kern County warriors who perished as a result of their service in Afghanistan or Iraq since September 11, 2001. Their portraits hang in the gallery. They are listed in chronological order by dates of death.)

1. Brian "Cody" Prosser (Army / December 5, 2001/ Afghanistan)

2. Troy Jenkins (Marine Corps & Army / April 24, 2003 / Iraq)

3. Osbaldo Orozco (Army / April 25, 2003 / Iraq)

4. David Perry (Army / August 10, 2003 / Iraq)

5. Marvin Sprayberry (Army / May 3, 2004 / Iraq)

6. Fernando Hannon (Marine Corps / August 15, 2004 / Iraq)

7. Ramon Villatoro Jr. (Army / July 24, 2005 / Iraq)

8. Clay Patrick Farr (Army / February 26, 2006 / Iraq)

9. Adam O. Zanutto (Marine Corps / March 6, 2006 / Iraq)

10. Richardo Barraza (Army / March 18, 2006)

11. Domenico Baroncini Jr. (Army / October 15, 2006 / Iraq)

12. Rudy Salcido (Army / November 9, 2006 / Iraq)

13. Angel Ramirez (Army / November 11, 2006 / Iraq)

14. Brian Freeman (Army / January 20, 2007 / Iraq)

15. Alberto Garcia Jr. (Army / March 13, 2007 / Iraq)

16. Rhys Klasno (Army / May 13, 2007 / Iraq)

17. Christopher Moore (Army / May 19, 2007 / Iraq)

18. Luis Gutierrez-Rosales (Army / July 18, 2007 / Iraq)

19. Benjamin Portell (Army / December 26, 2007 / Iraq)

20. Jason George (Army / May 21, 2009 / Iraq)

21. Joshua Soto (Army / June 16, 2009 / Iraq)

22. Brian Pedro (Army / October 2, 2010 / Afghanistan)

23. Joseph Lopez (Marine Corps / October 14, 2010 / Afghanistan)

24. Brett Land (Army / October 30, 2010 / Afghanistan)

25. Kenneth Hermogino (Air Force & Army / May 9, 2011 / Afghanistan)

26. Adan Gonzales Jr. (Marine Corps / August 7, 2011 / Afghanistan)

27. Herman Mackey III (Air Force / May 3, 2013 / Kyrgyzstan [supporting operations in Afghanistan])

Appendix 5:

D-Day 75th Anniversary Talk
By Craig W.H. Luther

Kern County Museum (June 5, 2019)

1. Introduction:

Normandy France is a pastoral land of fields, cows, ubiquitous apple orchards and farmhouses that produced milk, butter, and Camembert cheese. In 1944, the villages were mostly built of stone, and the region sprinkled with sturdy Romanesque and Gothic churches. It really is a charming place—the farmsteads with their terra cotta roofs are particularly so—and I've visited there on a half dozen occasions—researching the Normandy campaign and acting as a tour guide for both the 40th and 50th Anniversaries of the invasion in 1984 and 1994, respectively. The latter visit was particularly meaningful to me—we sat on bleachers on Omaha Beach—the Allied code name for the Normandy beach that was only secured with the loss of so much American blood. Sitting right before us, at the water's very edge, were most of the leaders of the free world: U.S President Clinton, President Mitterand of France, the Queen of England, and Lech Walesa (who had founded the Solidarity Movement in Poland that helped bring about the collapse of the Soviet Union), to name a few. And for me, to imagine what had happened here, precisely 50 years to the day—it gave me goosebumps and made me feel somehow connected to that Longest Day, as a book and a Hollywood movie described it, in a most intimate way.

And what about that day? June 6, 1944? Let me begin by introducing you to Tech Sgt Felix Branham, who landed with "K" Company, 116th Infantry Regiment. Late on D-Day, Tech Sgt. Branham, having survived the horror, chaos and death of the landing and made his way inland, returned to the beach at Omaha. He recalled: "It was shocking to see how many men were washing in the surf and many of them K Coy. Men I grew up with, caddied with, double-dated together, puffed off the same cigarette, drank out of the same bottle, lying there dead. Stark faces with eyes and mouths open, stone cold dead. It went through my mind that we were brothers, always would be. They died so we might live."

2. D-Day (6 Jun 44): The Story of The Longest Day

It all began shortly after midnight. Parachutists and glider-borne paratroopers were dropped at both ends of the Allied landing zone—to seize key objectives and to protect the flanks of the invasion forces against the anticipated (and inevitable) German counterattacks. Without getting ahead of the story, I should point out that the drop of the American paratrooper and glider forces went rather badly—or so it was thought at first. The crews of the American transport planes were inexperienced and knocked off course by German flak and poor navigation; as a result, many of the airborne troops missed their drop zones and were scattered over wide regions. However, as was later determined, this actually had the salutary effect of greatly confusing German commanders on the ground, who, with paratroopers appearing seemingly everywhere, were unsure where to focus their efforts.

While the Allied airborne forces were being deployed, the largest invasion armada of all time was plunging through the turbulent waters of the English Channel from its bases in southern England toward the

D-DAY 50

NORTHERN IRELAND EDITION

1D THE STARS AND STRIPES 1D

Daily Newspaper of U.S. Armed Forces in the European Theater of Operations

Vol. 1. No. 155. New York, N.Y.—Belfast, Northern Ireland. Tuesday, June 6, 1944.

INVASION!

Allies Chase Nazis Across River Tiber In Italy Advance

King Transfers Royal Powers To Crown Prince Umberto

The victorious Allied armies pursued the beaten remnants of the Wehrmacht across the River Tiber and up the main highways to the north yesterday after completing the occupation of Rome.

Some 500 heavy bombers joined lighter planes in smashing the enemy's escape routes and communication lines north of the capital. A Reuter correspondent reported that the Nazis' jammed convoys are paying a fearful price 50 or 60 miles north of Rome"

The Germans fled so fast that the Allied ground forces apparently could not keep in contact with them and no important fighting was reported during the day. They could not outdistance the Allied Air Force, however, and the planes destroyed 1,200 enemy vehicles on roads to the north.

In accordance with the proclamation he issued last April King Victor Emmanuel of Italy yesterday signed over his royal powers to the Crown Prince Umberto, who will take over

Aviation Output Exceeded Goal

ALLIES LAND IN FRANCE

Supreme Headquarters Allied Expeditionary Force announced this morning that Allied naval forces, supported by Allied air forces, began landing Allied armies this morning on the northern coast of France.

The official communique states'—

"Under the command of General Eisenhower, Allied naval forces, supported by strong air forces, began landing Allied armies this morning on the northern coast of France."

The communique was issued by Supreme Head-

Forts, Libs Hit Calais, Boulogne

The daily newspaper of U.S. forces in Europe on June 6, 1944.

Normandy coast—more than 6000 vessels, including 4000 landing craft, hundreds of "attack transports," and a bombardment force of 7 battleships, 2 monitors, 23 cruisers and 104 destroyers. Incredibly, German intelligence missed the armada because the inclement weather had grounded the German Air Force (GAF) and naval patrol boats. Of course, while one cannot say for sure, perhaps it was an act of Providence?

What was the atmosphere among the troops crammed into the transports of the Allied invasion fleet—among the men who, as one historian put it, were about to land on the edge of eternity? Who were acutely aware that, in a few short hours, they might well be dispatched into eternity? Many of the men had a resigned, somber mood—some read, some wrote letters to loved ones, some played craps or card games, but most remained silent, lost in their own private thoughts. "An invasion ship is a lonely ship," noted an American sergeant, below deck on one of the thousands of landing craft. "You sit and sweat and nobody says anything because there is nothing to say. . . You look around and you wonder who will be dead soon."

Several hours later, a staggering aerial bombardment began. By June 1944, Allied airpower dominated the skies over Western Europe; indeed, as the Supreme Commander of the invasion forces, General Dwight D. Eisenhower, stated, "without air supremacy, I wouldn't be here." Thousands of American and British bombers, as well as fighter planes festooned with deadly rockets, struck key German positions along the Normandy coastline, softening them up for the ground invasion to come.

The first landing craft launched from their transports at about 4.00 a.m., amidst dark, heavy cloud cover and choppy seas. All told, elements of six divisions (3 American, 2 British, 1 Canadian) were to be landed along a patch of the Normandy coastline stretching for some 50 miles. As the late historian Sir John Keegan observed, the plan of attack, that is, the tactical scheme, was surprisingly simple and general. As one colonel put it, "We are not being cute, no gimmicks, no flanking movements. We are coming straight at him with everything we have. This is strictly power." That said, the initial waves of the assault were regarded as virtually "suicidal." Recalled a private who took part in the assault on Omaha Beach: "We were told that we would probably all be killed." This ramped up the tension among the men, so that "the night before was like waiting to go to the electric chair."

The Germans had committed three divisions to this sector of the Normandy coast, but only one was a good, battle-tested formation. In general, the Germans suffered from serious shortages of everything from manpower to motor fuel—the long, bloody war in the East having drained the German Army of many of its best officers and men, not to mention most of its tanks, artillery, and other heavy weapons. All told, the forces in the West included a number of excellent armored and infantry divisions, but a large number of the 58 divisions there were second-rate formations. The GAF (Luftwaffe) was also seriously depleted and would be able to do little to help in the face of immense Anglo-American air superiority. And yet the coastline bristled with the fixed defenses of Hitler's vaunted Atlantic Wall—a network of fortifications that included heavy artillery within massive concrete bunkers, pillboxes, machine-gun nests, underground troop shelters, and all manner of diabolical beach obstacles ranging from the coast of German-occupied Holland across Belgium and France.

If I may briefly digress: It was Field Marshal Erwin Rommel, the famed Desert Fox of the German Afrika Korps, who was responsible for the defense of the French coastline. Rommel's unpleasant experiences with Allied air power in North Africa had convinced him it would be all but impossible to hurl the Allies back into the sea once they had gained a foothold on the coast. Allied fighters and bombers, so went his thinking, enjoying complete air superiority, were bound to destroy German tank reserves advancing toward the beaches to repel the landings, while Allied naval gunfire would also prevent the Germans from regaining the coastline. Thus, he was firmly convinced the only strategy available to him was to defeat the invasion at the water's edge.

Since taking over command of Army Group B and its two armies in France at the end of 1943, Rommel had redoubled efforts to strengthen the Atlantic Wall. For example, within a few weeks of his arrival in France, mine laying had increased from about 40,000 to more than one million a month, and, by May 20, 1944, over 4,000,000 mines

German "Hedgehog" Beach Defenses Normandy, France (May 6, 1944)
(USMC Archives from Quantico, USA, CC BY 2.0, via Wikimedia Commons)

were in place; moreover, between November 1943 and May 1944, a half million obstacles were positioned on the beaches and likely airborne landing zones. And yet, when the Allied invasion began, the Atlantic Wall was only about 20% complete in the Normandy region. On June 6, however, Rommel, assured that bad weather ruled out an invasion for the time being, was not at his HQ at La Roche Guyon, but at home in Germany, planning to confer with the "Führer" to plead for reinforcements for his forces Normandy.

And what of the German defenders hunkered down in their bunkers and firing positions behind the Normandy beaches? How did they react to the sudden appearance of the largest, most powerful invasion fleet the world had ever witnessed?

Just before sunrise, German Lt. Hans Heinz was looking out of his treetop observation post overlooking the town Colleville, just inland from Omaha Beach. The sea was covered in mist. "Then a light breeze came up," he recalled. "First, we saw a great number of mastheads, just like asparagus poking out of the thin mist. A few minutes later, the wind tore the fog away completely. I will never forget the spine-chilling scene that met our eyes. At first, I thought it was a vision, but shortly after I grasped the awful reality of the scenario. There were thousands of ships. . . It was as if the whole world was standing against us."

"The whole situation was unfolding in a way that seemed almost like a dream, detached from reality," said another German soldier. "This great assembly of ships was simply looming out of the sea mist, just getting bigger and bigger, closer and closer. . . I had a great sensation that we were on our own in front of this colossal force. . . It was unnerving but I also felt a certain relief, even excitement, that at last we would meet this enemy that threatened us."

Between 6.00-7.30 a.m., the landing craft shepherding the initial waves of the American, British and Canadian forces began reach the coastline. The craft carrying the first waves were launched 8-12 miles out to sea; the ride in lasted 1.5-2 hours and most all of the men became seasick in the choppy, tumultuous waters; others suffered from hypothermia. And still, in most sectors—certainly in the British and Canadian landing zones—the invasion came off well; German resistance was often weak, even negligible in some areas, and troops, tanks, guns and vehicles disgorged from their transports began to move tentatively inland.

Yet on Omaha Beach, the story was much different, so terribly different. U.S. GIs, men of the battle-hardened 1st Infantry Division (the "Big Red One"), supported by elements of the 29th Infantry Division, an untested National Guard unit, ran headlong into a first-class German infantry division (the 352nd, whose presence on the Normandy coast had been missed by Allied intelligence); as a result, they were pinned down on the beach for hours, literally paralyzed, unable to move, their losses enormous. One company of 155 men quickly suffered 100 dead, virtually all the remainder wounded. Nineteen of the dead

"Into the Jaws of Death:" Soldiers of 1st Infantry Division disembark on Omaha Beach (June 6, 1944)

(Chief Photographer's Mate (CPHOM) Robert F. Sargent, U.S. Coast Guard, Public domain, via Wikimedia Commons)

came from one small rural community in the town of Bedford, VA; including two sets of brothers. The G.I.s were exhausted by seasickness and disoriented by hypothermia. They were also overloaded with too much equipment; some couldn't shoot as their rifles were clogged with sand. They were caught on the open beach with nowhere to hide and cut to pieces by withering pre-registered fire from German artillery, AT guns, mortars and MGs—the artillery shells slamming into the beach at nearly three times the speed of sound. Some of the officers who were still alive on the beach thought the invasion had already failed.

The preternatural horror of this day at Omaha Beach defies adequate description. Hundreds of dead bodies were afloat in the surf; hundreds more lay on the beach, along with the body parts of men dismembered by enemy fire. The wounds sustained by men struck at close range by modern weapons of war were often gruesome. One Pharmacist's Mate was almost reduced to tears by the fearful state of some of the returning wounded. "Never have I seen such suffering," he averred. "The wounds were terrible. One man lay quietly on a litter smoking a cigarette, with five machine gun wounds in his chest. Another had one of his buttocks shot off, exposing six inches of the huge sciatic nerve."

Only due to the courage and daring actions of small groups of men, were the G.I.s gradually able to break the stalemate on the beach, surmount the bluffs overlooking the beach, and begin to knock out German strongpoints that had wreaked so much havoc for so long. Many of these brave men didn't survive D-Day, and so their heroic acts died with them, never to be recorded for posterity.

Also helping to turn the tide on Omaha Beach was the courageous action of U.S. Navy destroyers off the coast. By late morning, they were closing to point blank range—so close to the beach that their hulls nearly scraped bottom. The destroyers pumped shell after shell out of their 5-inch guns, neutralizing key German strongpoints.

As the men finally got off the beach and scaled the 150-200 foot high bluffs, they became enmeshed in dreadful hand-to-hand fighting. Recalled one German soldier: "The ferocity of the fighting astonished me. Men were lunging at each other with fixed bayonets, and with their rifle stocks, and even with entrenching tools or shovels. The Americans were charging upon our German gunners in the barbed wire entanglements up there. Some men were in flames, and other men were shooting or stabbing them as they staggered on fire."

By early afternoon, what had initially appeared to be a major German victory at Omaha, was slowly turning into a hard-fought success for the battered and bloodied Americans. Adolf Hitler, however, unaware of the unprecedented size and scope of the Allied invasion effort, was bursting with confidence. As he informed one of his top generals that day: "As long as they were in Britain, we couldn't get at them. Now we have them where we can destroy them." Yet in the days and weeks ahead, Hitler's confidence would be no match for the overwhelming might of the Allied invaders.

By the end of D-Day, the stalwart GIs of the "Big Red One," supported by the National Guardsmen of 29th Infantry Division, had carved out a modest beachhead that was barely 1.4 miles deep at the farthest penetration; it was a tenuous foothold, but a foothold it was (even if it was the smallest of the five beachheads achieved on D-Day).

By the conclusion of June 6, 1944, more than 150,000 Allied troops were ashore in Normandy. Supported by specialized armored units, as well as the devastating firepower of Allied air and naval units, the assault divisions of the invasion force had cleaved deep chunks from Hitler's vaunted Atlantic Wall. In the skies above Normandy, Allied dominance was absolute. On D-Day, Allied strategic and tactical air forces flew 10,585 sorties, while the Germans managed barely more than 300.

Yet Allied forces had paid a steep price for their success, with American, British, and Canadian casualties amounting to more than 10,000 men.

Landing ships put cargo ashore on Omaha Beach early in the campaign.
(Original uploader MickStephenson at English Wikipedia, Public domain, via Wikimedia Commons)

Of course, by far the greatest of these losses were at Omaha Beach, where the Americans sustained several thousand casualties including well over 1000 fatal losses.

Let me tell you the story of just one of those brave men who perished on Omaha Beach. It is the story of a soldier who will forever remain anonymous to history. It was later in the day. The battle had finally turned in the Americans' favor. Kurt Keller, a German soldier, armed only with his rifle, and feeling increasingly vulnerable to the enormous odds again him and his comrades, suddenly saw an American soldier coming directly toward him. With trembling hands, Keller quickly aimed at the G.I.'s chest and pulled the trigger: "The American was left standing, let his rifle drop, and sank to his knees. Slowly taking his helmet off, he laid it on the rifle and looking up to the sky, he crossed himself and fell over on his face." The image was to haunt Keller forever: "How could a man be so devout and believe in God at that moment?" he recalled thinking. "Hitler was my god, until then."

Yet despite such losses, despite counterattacks mounted by the

Germans in a desperate attempt to hurl the Anglo-American invaders back into the sea, the landing had succeeded. And with the success of the landing, the western allies had grabbed a toe hold in France from which they were not to be extruded.

Now began the fight in the so-called Bocage country for the Americans. Massive hedgerows were the backbone of this soon to be infamous and bloody terrain, for which the G.I., oddly enough, had not been trained. The hedgerows were field boundaries planted by the Celtic farmers 2000 years earlier. Over two millennia, their entangled roots had collected earth to form banks as much as 10 feet thick. To the Germans, they offered almost impregnable defensive

American G.I.'s move through a breach in the hedgerows in Normandy.
(Unknown American soldier, Public domain, via Wikimedia Commons)

positions—force multipliers at intervals of just 100 to 200 yards; to the attacking American infantry, they posed death traps. Step by step, however, over the intervening weeks, the Germans were slowly pushed back and, eventually, overcome by the overpowering might of Anglo-American military power on land, sea, and in the air.

The American breakout from Normandy began in late July 1944, and in August, in cooperation with British and Canadian forces, the remnants of Hitler's armies in Normandy were entrapped and obliterated. Allied ground forces now began to race through France toward the German frontier. Paris was liberated. It seemed that the Germans would never recover and that the war might be over by Christmas. But recover they did, and fierce and bloody fighting would go on for many more months—from Arnhem, to Hurtgen Forest, to the Battle of the Bulge—until Nazi Germany finally capitulated in May 1945.

3. Conclusion:

Yet that is a story for another day. More to the point, what can be said about the significance of the Allied victory at Normandy on June 6, 1944?

Simply put, with the success of the Normandy landings, the fate of Hitler's "1000-year Reich" was finally sealed. The Anglo-Americans had established a major second front in Europe, relieving pressure on the Soviet Union, which had been fighting the bulk of the German Army for three years, and had suffered indescribably as a result. Germany was now fighting a war on two major fronts (and a secondary front in Italy) with limited and declining resources—it was a war she could not win. In fact, by June 1944, fully 75% of the world's resources had been mobilized against the Axis powers (primarily Germany and Japan)—thus, their total defeat was simply a matter of time. And defeat came, as noted, in May 1945 for Germany; in September 1945 for Japan.

Yet let us also contemplate the unthinkable: What if the invasion had failed? Observes one historian: "If an Allied repulse on D-Day did not actually lead to some form of victory for Hitler, at best it would have meant another costly year of war, ruinous for Britain, the extinction of the last remaining remnants of European Jewry through

Destroyed German Panzer IV tank in Normandy.
(Connolly (Sgt), No 5 Army Film & Photographic Unit, Public domain, via Wikimedia Commons)

completion of the Final Solution, culminating almost certainly with the employment of the first atomic bombs in the summer of 1945—on Germany, not Japan. Sweeping through a 'nuked' Germany, the victorious Red Army would have stopped nowhere short of the Rhine. Lost to Communism, Europe, and the world, would have been a very different place today."

Seventy-five years have now passed since D-Day, and the overwhelming majority of the gallant young men who stormed the beaches of Normandy against such frightful odds have now departed this world. But forgotten? No, they are not forgotten. Five U.S. Presidents, beginning with Jimmy Carter in 1978, have visited Normandy, toured the battlefields, and paid homage to the heroes of that extraordinary day.

On June 6, 1984, President Ronald Reagan stood above Omaha Beach and delivered his iconic address about the "Boys of Pointe de Hoc." These were the elite U.S. Rangers, who had scaled the 9-story high cliffs to destroy a German gun battery that, it was feared, would wreak havoc on the Americans at Omaha Beach. The guns, it turned out, had already been moved to another location, but the attacking Rangers, 225 men in all, fought so tenaciously against such bitter German resistance that barely 90 were still in action after just 48 hours.

On June 6, 2004, the 60th Anniversary of the invasion, President George W. Bush opined: “That road to V-E Day was hard and long, and traveled by weary and valiant men. And history will always record where that road began. It began here, with the first footprints on the beaches of Normandy.”

The iconic nature of America’s D-Day experience has also been immortalized by Hollywood—by director Darryl F. Zanuck’s film, *The Longest Day* (based on the book with the same title by Cornelius Ryan); and, of course, in 1998, by Steven Spielberg’s graphically realistic portrayal, *Saving Private Ryan.*

In other words, the dreadful, bloody—yet without question—necessary events of June 6, 1944 (and the months that followed) remain to this day an integral part of our unique American experience, of our history, our folklore, and, certainly, of our immense pride as a peace-loving people. We liberated the French people from Nazi oppression, and tens of thousands of our soldiers died doing so. And all we asked for in return were a few patches of hallowed soil in which to bury our dead.

As American novelist and poet Barbara Kingsolver once observed: “There’s a graveyard in northern France where all the dead boys from D-Day are buried. The white crosses reach from one horizon to the other. I remember looking it over and thinking it was a forest of graves. But the rows were like this, dizzying, diagonal, perfectly straight, so after all it wasn’t a forest but an orchard of graves. Nothing to do with nature, unless you count human nature.”

That graveyard is located on a bluff overlooking Omaha Beach and the English Channel. It covers 172.5 acres and contains the remains of 9,388 American military dead, most of whom were killed during

The American Military Cemetery above Omaha Beach

the invasion of Normandy and ensuing operations in the European theater. It is a hallowed patch of sovereign U.S. soil on French ground. I've visited this sacred place on several occasions. I would urge you to do so as well—if only to remind yourself that freedom isn't free, and that the freedoms we all enjoy today—and, too often, take for granted—are due to the brave men resting eternally beneath those white crosses.

So, please, let me conclude by once more recalling the words of TechSgt Felix Branham; because now, now that you all know a little more about the heroism, the suffering and dying on that Longest Day, his words should resonate even more: "It was shocking," he said, "to see how many men were washing in the surf and many of them K Coy. Men I grew up with, caddied with, double-dated together, puffed off the same cigarette, drank out of the same bottle, lying there dead. Stark faces with eyes and mouths open, stone cold dead. It went through my mind that we were brothers, always would be. They died so we might live."

Key Sources:

Eckhertz, Holger. *D-Day through German Eyes* (DTZ History Publications, 2015).

I.C.B. Dear (ed.). *The Oxford Companion to World War II* (Oxford University Press, 1st Edition, 1995).

Keegan, John. *The Second World War* (Viking/Penguin, 1989).

Kershaw, Robert. *Landing on the Edge of Eternity. Twenty-four Hours at Omaha Beach.* (Pegasus Books, 2018).

Luther, Craig. *Blood and Honor. The History of the 12th SS Panzer-Division "Hitler Youth," 1943/1945* (Schiffer Books, 2012).

Weinberg, Gerhard. *A World At Arms. A Global History of World War II* (Cambridge University Press, 1994).

Acknowledgments

I am acutely aware that, without the support and encouragement of literally dozens of folks, this book project would never have seen the light of day. Let me tell you about some of these wonderful people.

Let me begin with Mrs. Claudia Needham-White, owner/publisher of "The Loop Newspaper" in Tehachapi. As I explained in my preface, it was with Claudia that the idea originated to do articles on local veterans in her newspaper. Thus, in a very big way, we all owe this book to her love and support of those men and women who have served our country over the past three generations.

To those living veterans, whose stories make up the majority of this book—you deserve very special praise. You gave generously of your time and were remarkably patient in the face of my merciless interrogations, as I plied you with question after question to coax out your stories. In cases where the veterans are deceased (e.g., all my WWII stories [Part One], three of my Iraq stories [Part Four]), I could not have composed the articles without the gracious and patient support of their devoted family members—a wife, two wonderful mothers, a father, and, in one instance, a son. I will never know just how difficult it must have been for all of you to relive such ineffably tragic and painful experiences, but I honor and salute you for your courage to do so.

To *all* of the veterans—living and deceased—who grace the pages of "Our Soldiers' Stories," let me say this: You are among the chosen few—you are the ones who made a beeline to the recruiting stations after the Japanese bombed Pearl Harbor on December 7, 1941, or after Al-Qaeda terrorists used commercial airliners as missiles to kill thousands of Americans on September 11, 2001; you are the nurses who pulled 12-hour shifts, six-days-a-week in Vietnam, caring selflessly for the wounded and the dying. Yet, most of all, you are the ones who put service to country above self, who risked everything—and, in several cases, lost everything—so that others could lead comfortable lives in our country, safe and free. I know it has become a cliché of sorts, but let me repeat it still: Thank you for your service to our great country. You are America's finest treasure.

I would be remiss if I did not acknowledge the following folks for their indispensable support of this book project. Dr. David Day, a dear friend who was at my side every step of the way, shared ideas and offered encouragement on an almost daily basis and, perhaps most significantly, let me know by the example he set that I was not carrying the burden of the effort alone. Ms. Lili Maish, the founder of Honor Flights Kern County, and co-founder of the Portrait of a Warrior Gallery in Bakersfield, was an enthusiastic supporter of this project from its inception. I cannot thank her enough for helping to make this book a reality. Sgt. Maj. (ret.) Jason M. Geis, MBA (U.S. Army), Executive Director and co-founder of the Portrait of a Warrior Gallery, also provided some key help when I needed it most. Mr. Alex Athans (U.S. Army, ret.), Quarter Master, Jason E. George VFW Post 12114, played a crucial role in locating veterans for me to interview; as did Jed Hannan (U.S. Navy, ret.). I am indebted to them both. Let me also thank Dr. Jonathan Roth, Director of the Charles B. Burdick Military History Project (San Jose State University), for his encouragement and for helping to get the message out for fundraising purposes.

If money, as a politician once opined, is the "mother's milk of politics," it is no less vital to a project such as this one. Simply put, without the generous financial support of dozens of individuals and organizations—most notable among them Lili Maish and Jason Geis (Portrait of a Warrior Gallery), Ed Wette, Todd Schultz, John Pruden, and Valley Baptist Church—I would have gotten nowhere. (For a complete list of financial contributors, please see the "Contributors Honor Role" directly below.)

It is with endless gratitude that I mention Mrs. Lara Steinke, a highly-skilled English teacher who, at the last minute, when time was short, took on the final edit of my manuscript, saving me from more typographical and spelling errors than I will ever acknowledge. Her marvelous effort raised up my book to a new level of editorial perfection. I even learned about an "animal" known as a "compound predicate!" Who knew?

The layout of the book, preparing it for publication, was accomplished by the very talented and delightful Ms. Sara Olsher. She helped us to create something special, and I cannot thank her enough for that. And "kudos" to Barry Bongberg (U.S. Army Vietnam veteran) for recommending Sara to me. I should add that Barry recently published an outstanding work on Vietnam that I would recommend to anyone interested in our experience there: *Dear Mom & Dad. Letters Home from Vietnam, 1967-1969*.

Also helping to make this book something special are the many photographs furnished by the veterans and/or their families. All of their photographs used in this book are captioned with "Photo Provided." Other photographs were gleaned to the best of my knowledge from non-proprietary sources, such as the U.S. National

Archives, Wikimedia Commons, and other internet sites that permit free public use.

As always, I thank my dear (and long suffering) wife of more than 20 years, Therese Luther, who helped to edit all 25 of the stories while offering her love and encouragement. Once again, she graciously accepted life with an "absentee" husband, hunkered down in his study for hours at a time and often not getting to bed until 1.00 or 2.00 in the morning. We've gone through this many times, dear, but this may well be the last time. So your almost preternatural patience may have finally paid off! But then again?

Contributors Honor Roll

Individuals:

Raul Alvarez

Alex & Patricia Athans

Bill Beasley

Barry Bongberg (Platinum Contributor)*

Steven & Doni Bowersox

Dieter & Connie Brehm (Platinum Contributor)

Chuck Cournyea

David & Kathy Day

Dennis & Sandra Fernandez

Michael Gillum

John & Shawnee Gongola

Jed Hannan

Neill & Andi Hicks

David Howell

Craig & Therese Luther (Platinum Contributor)

Robert Luther

Ross & MacKenzie McGuire

Joseph T. McNaught

Thomas Morris

Bill Norton (Platinum Contributor)

James E. O'Donnell

Adam Oke

Jerry Brevier & Lorraine Oke

John Pruden (Platinum Contributor)

Phoebe Racine

David and Kathy Rheinhart

Michele Slade

Lauraine Snelling

Pamela Stacks

Brian & Julie Stainfield

Lee & Diane Tharp

Mark Yarlot

Rick & Donna Zanutto (Platinum Contributor)

Businesses & Other Organizations:

Dr. Beverley Billingsley (Billingsley Veterinarian Clinic)

Valley Baptist Church (Bakersfield / Platinum Contributor)

Jason E. George VFW Post 12114 (Tehachapi)

Paul Hearn (Hearn Drilling)

Jess Lopez (A Barber Shop)

Marty Pay (Farmers Insurance Agency)

Jean-Luc Sabourin (Shelby Pumps & Well Service, Inc.)

Todd Schultz (Golden Age Flight Museum / Platinum Contributor)

Portrait of a Warrior Gallery (Bakersfield / Platinum Contributor)

Ed Wette (N.E.W. Luxury Vehicles, LLC / Platinum Contributor)

*Contribution of $250 or more.

My sincere apology to anyone who contributed after October 7, 2021, and thus is not on this list.

About the Author

Dr. Craig W.H. Luther was awarded his doctorate degree in Modern European History (emphasis Nazi Germany 1933/45) from U.C. Santa Barbara in 1987. He was a civilian historian in the U.S. Air Force for 27 years—16 years at McClellan AFB, outside Sacramento, California; and 11 years at Edwards AFB, in the high desert of Southern California. He is also a Fulbright Scholar (Bonn, West Germany, 1979/80) and author of eight books on World War II. His most recent WWII books include: *Blood and Honor: The History of the 12th SS Panzer-Division "Hitler Youth," 1933-1945* (1988/second edition with new material 2012); *Barbarossa Unleashed: The German Blitzkrieg through Central Russia to the Gates of Moscow, June-December 1941* (2014); and, T*he First Day on the Eastern Front: Germany Invades the Soviet Union, June 22, 1941* (2018). He is recognized internationally as an expert scholar on Operation *Barbarossa*, Adolf Hitler's surprise attack on Soviet Russia, the most gigantic, monstrous, and costly war the world has ever witnessed. His WWII books can be purchased directly from Amazon, traditional "brick and mortar" book retailers, or directly from him: luther.craig@yahoo.com, or (661) 303-8884.

www.ingramcontent.com/pod-product-compliance
Lightning Source LLC
LaVergne TN
LVHW081259100826
845148LV00005B/918
9781736611470